ENDORSEMENTS FOR STERLING

"I thought, 'Why would anyone write for Hollywood?' After I met Sterling Anderson, that changed. I began to explore writing for television. He generously guided me through the whole process of the art in the craft. At first glance you knew he was right about everything. Most importantly, he wasn't a charlatan hocking tired and used shortcut methods to make it in Hollywood so I could have a house in Malibu with a Playmate/Playboy. He was a thoughtful, empathetic, generous, and a deeply intuitive teacher. **Honestly, I credit him for starting off my career writing for television.**"

—*Josh Miller, Screenwriter*

"Not only did Sterling give me brilliant, incisive advice on my script, he believed in my rewrite enough to forward it to his manager. I learned more in an hour talking to Sterling than I had in the last five years of webcasts and seminars on screenwriting. He discussed my script with a level of detail I hadn't considered before. **The guy is a real pro.**"

—*Ed Gaus, The Chicago Screenwriter's Network*

"It's pretty easy to get lost in the world of Hollywood, where anyone and everyone has an opinion and 'words of advice'—Sterling's are actually the kind you want to listen to. As a graduate student at USC's School of Cinematic Arts, I learned more in one class with Sterling than most students can hope for during their entire schooling. From feature films to television, and everything in between, **Sterling taught me to be a better writer, director, and overall story teller.**"

—*Matthew MacDonald, USC School of Cinematic Arts*

D0311339

Books by Sterling Anderson

Writing Without Fear
15 Steps Toward Becoming a Successful (Artist) Writer

Beyond Screenwriting: Insider Tips and Career Advice from
a Successful Hollywood TV and Film Writer

Does He Cheat?
Confessions from Men: 50 Signs Your Partner May Be Cheating

BEYOND SCREENWRITING:

Insider Tips and Career Advice from a Successful Hollywood TV and Film Writer

by

Sterling Anderson

with

Andrea Goss Knaub

DEDICATION

David Mamet taught me how to write. Sidney Poitier taught me that class and dignity outrank most human qualities. Robert Greenwald taught me that you're no one unless you give back to the less fortunate and underprivileged. Charles Dutton told me emphatically to be myself when I write. Coretta Scott King sat in her kitchen and told me stories of immeasurable fortitude.

I've had great mentors for whom I will always be grateful.

All my love to Asa, Maia, Adrian, Kareem, Cameron, Inigo, Artemis, Lauryn, and Isley.

TABLE OF CONTENTS

PREFACE

Beyond Screenwriting originated from Sterling Anderson's screenwriting workshops and his experience teaching undergraduate and graduate students at University of Southern California's School of Cinematic Arts, where students would consistently ask, "What book on screenwriting do you recommend?" Sterling did not know how to answer the question because a great majority of screenwriting books are written by authors who have not sold screenplays, been hired to write screenplays (by WGA signatories), or had any experience in a writers' room on a television series. Like many subjects, there is a vast difference between theory and application.

One of Sterling's students, Andrea Goss Knaub, an editor and writer, suggested he write a book based on practical experiences from his 18 years of being a paid Hollywood screenwriter. Sterling sat down with Andrea to compile a list of common questions asked by aspiring screenwriters. The result is a book Sterling and Andrea call *Beyond Screenwriting* because it delves into "real world" insider information beyond the basics most screenplay books cover (i.e., formatting), such as how to get your screenplay read and what to expect on your first day in the writers' room. This book gives readers a peek behind the curtain of the life of a Hollywood writer, and what writers need to know and do to get in—and succeed.

Beyond Screenwriting is a book based more on questions and practical answers rather than the author's beliefs and theories. It is a book for all students, aspiring writers, and current writers who want to know more. In fact, this book wouldn't be possible without the curious minds of Sterling's students. Special thanks are extended to every student who asked questions beneficial to all writers, and to institutions like USC School of Cinematic Arts, Columbia College film school, Zaki Gordon Film Institute, Eastern Michigan University, and all colleges, high schools, and even coffee shop conversations that focus on good writing.

Appreciation is also extended to all writers, producers, directors, assistant directors, actors, cinematographers, script supervisors, sound and lighting engineers, and editors who have all had something resourceful to say about storytelling. To all, thank you.

S.A. and A.G.K.

INTRODUCTION

I decided to steal time between screenwriting jobs to write a book about the craft because the most popular question from my students is, "What screenwriting book should I buy?"

Every time I hear this question, I think of the plethora of screenwriting books on the market. I have not thumbed through many of these books in several years. When I taught at USC School of Cinematic Arts, we were required to have a reading list at the beginning of every semester. My required reading list on screenwriting has never wavered. I've only recommended three books in five years of university adjunct professorship: Ann Lamont's *Bird by Bird,* Stephen King's *On Writing: A Memoir of the Craft,* and Frederick Raphael's *Eyes Wide Shut.*

I have no profound reason why these are my favorites. They just appeal to me. None of these books are instructional in screenwriting, although Frederick Raphael's *Eyes Wide Shut* is one of the most truthful accounts of what it is actually like to be a screenwriter.

Several people and students endorse different screenwriting books with enthusiasm. I have been asked, "Have you read this one or have you read that one?" No, I haven't. I'm a professional screenwriter with screenwriting credits. I don't read books on screenwriting. One reason is I don't have time. The other reason is because most of these books are written by failed screenwriters, or worse, by people who have never written or sold a screenplay at all.

There are two major reasons most screenwriting books have not been written by professional screenwriters. One, most of them are too busy writing screenplays or pounding the pavement trying to get hired to write a screenplay. The second reason is that the film and television business is a fear-based industry. Many professional screenwriters believe if they teach screenwriting, or write a book about it, they are taking up time that could be spent writing scripts, thereby increasing their chances of someone taking their next job. I have not done a survey, but this latter reason is based on my experience in network and studio story meetings and television writing rooms. Professional screenwriters realize we are but a moment away from getting fired, so we need to always stay on top of our game.

Job security is not any reason to get into this business. Neither is ego. During my first job on a one-hour television series, I asked a seasoned writer how not to get fired. He said, "It's impossible not to get fired. All screenwriters eventually get fired." I gave him my best disbelieving expression and went about my business. After that season I was fired.

The reason so many non-professional screenwriters write books about screenwriting is an enigma to me. Not many non-police officers write about or teach law enforcement. Even fewer non-professional firefighters teach firefighting. Would you take your child to a pediatrician who has never gone to medical school and practiced medicine? There is so much revenue generated on classes, screenwriting contests, and seminars—all by people who have never sold a screenplay, never been hired by a network or studio to write a screenplay, and never been a writer on a television show.

There are countless universities, colleges, junior colleges, and even high schools that hire people who have never sold a screenplay to teach screenwriting. This is understandable. There is a need, and the need has to be filled. I'm happy to report I have lectured at universities like Eastern Michigan and Columbia College of Chicago, where students were well informed and properly exposed to television and film writing. Many teachers are not professional screenwriters, but they have done their homework.

At the same time, it is hard for even competent educators to know the true ins and outs of the business unless they have been hired to write a movie or have been a staff writer on a television show. Even if I could build a race car from scratch with my eyes closed, that doesn't mean I could drive it during a race at Daytona 500. It helps to learn from someone who has been there, done that. Learning how to write a screenplay from a professional screenwriter raises the odds that you, too, can not only write a screenplay—but sell one, or two, or three, or more, to make a career of it as I have. The best teacher, though, is on-the-job training. Every job I have been paid to write, I have learned from someone. Every tedious story meeting where I feel like a wet paper towel when finished, I still learn.

Beyond Screenwriting goes beyond what anyone with an Internet connection can find and toss together as a screenwriting book. Enough non-pros are doing it.

This book goes behind the brick wall and into the inner sanctums of Hollywood—into the writers' rooms and producers' offices and studio meetings where the real business of screenwriting happens. I can take you there because I've been there, and I am there. This book is a compilation of what I've learned from my own experiences and from fellow screenwriters, directors, producers, and network and studio executives. These are things about screenwriting that other authors/writers who have never sold a screenplay or worked on a film or TV show couldn't possibly know.

I've been fortunate to work with award-winning actors, directors, producers, and even editors—who are the last writers on every film and television project. I've learned so much from sitting in on editing sessions. And by sharing what I've learned with you, I hope to give you a glimpse into the world you wish to enter—and a leg up in achieving success and avoiding common mistakes.

A friend of mine told me that the constraints and structure of screenwriting are too confining. This may be true of any profession. However, in order to break structure, you have to know structure. Every great tennis player hits the ball off the wrong foot, off balance, and without looking—but in order to do this, their fundamentals have to be impeccable. I challenge all writers to learn the rules well enough to break them correctly, and to learn screenwriting from someone (like me) who is successful at it. And then, stop reading, and write, write, write. Learn on the job. Go forth and conquer, and sit in the writers' room with me.

Now let's get started.

STORY

A great number of people have approached me over the years, or should I say "cornered me," to tell me they had the story to end all stories. Ninety percent of the time the preface has been, "Sterling, as a screenwriter, you should be so lucky to write the story I'm about to tell you." I've always tried to demonstrate manners and patience by taking a beat to finish whatever I was involved in: a conversation, a meal, a last bite of dessert, or a quick flush.

The tall tales over the years have ranged from, "My 95-year-old grandmother climbed Mount Everest in her bare feet," to "My long-lost twin was captured by wild natives, but managed to dive off a 500-foot cliff and swim down the Nile, to eventually be raised by gorillas in the mist." Whatever the story has been, most of them have been hair-raising and incredibly interesting. Unfortunately, very few of the tales have been a perfect fit for the big screen or television.

So what makes a story stand out as a possible Academy Award-winning screenplay? Is there a litmus test? Is there a key that unlocks the vault and catapults me to the computer to eagerly type "fade in"?

Most people think it's the big story: Armageddon, or World War V, or the fall of democracy. The big story is what people want to pitch, but what writers really should want to write is the small story.

Whatever the epic size of the canvas, it is the small story that more often than not is the glue to making an interesting story into a captivating story.

What is the small story?

Let us look at a large canvas like the Italian mafia family spanning through three generations. This is the large story, the big story. Then downsize that large story to a wayward son dedicated to never involving himself in the family mafia business. That son goes to Italy and meets the love of his life, the woman of his dreams. The new bride and groom have a romantic interlude filled with dance, wine, song, and tradition. Then the bride is accidentally murdered. The distraught new groom plans to exact his revenge. He leaps head-first into the complicated folds of his family mafia business, only to eventually become the head of that business.

This large story was called *The Godfather.*

This is a brilliant example of how the writer took on the large epic mafia drama, and then beautifully crafted a small story within the large story. The small story becomes the catalyst to ignite the large story and make it leap off the screen.

Another example of a writer who finds the small story within the large story is a tale of an innocent Amish boy who accidentally witnesses the execution of a man in the bathroom stall of a Philadelphia train station. The murderer spots the Amish boy and plans to track him back to the

Amish country. A big city police detective goes undercover to guard and protect the Amish boy against his eventual murder attempt. While the big city police detective is undercover with a group of people who are as foreign to him as he is to them, the writer crafted a smaller story within the large story. The writer had the big city detective fall in love with the boy's mother.

The large story was called *Witness.*

The writer crafted a wonderful small story that eventually breaks down all awkwardness and barriers between the big city culture and the small town Amish culture (as love always does).

Another small story within a large story is about teen pregnancy. The story is about a precarious, offbeat, teenage girl who decides she's going to coast through teen pregnancy without taking on the looks, ridicule, and judgment of peers and family. The writer skillfully crafted a small story of the precocious teen who meets the future (adoptive) father and mother of her unborn child. The teen discovers that the future father is suffering with his own self-esteem issues because he lives with a woman who refuses to see him or consider his needs. The teen has to realize that teen pregnancy isn't a coast through the whipped cream and strawberries of life. Her discovery leads her to consider how her pregnancy does have a domino effect on everyone in her arena. She has to grow up and take life more seriously.

The large story was called *Juno.*

The small story is how Juno realizes her future baby's parents are as flawed as her own.

The Godfather, Witness, and *Juno* are all different stories, but the common denominator is how the small stories weave and glue the large stories into beautiful cinematic mosaics.

Every time I set out to get a writing assignment, or sit down and write my own story, I always lock in on the small story. If I nail the small story, I know I can nail the larger story.

How does this work in television? Easy. When you sit down to develop a pilot that is self-contained (meaning the "A" story is wrapped up and finished at the end of the hour or half hour), remember that the most compelling part of the story is not always catching the bad guy. More often than not, it is the "B" and "C" story (the smaller stories) that is the glue that holds the episode together—and draws the viewers in.

On the series *The Unit,* our ratings did not only rely on the Delta Force setting off to complete their missions. When the show was tested, we received another large share of our ratings after viewers got interested in the ongoing relationships among the families, wives, children, and husbands: the smaller stories.

On *Medium,* it wasn't Allison's psychic ability to solve the crimes that drew the compassion of our viewers. We knew she was going to solve the crimes. It was how she dealt with her husband and children that brought the loyal viewers in every week: the smaller stories.

When I am one of the writers considered for a writing assignment in feature films, I know my interview depends on my "small story pitch" that lands me the job. For example, when Quincy Jones (producer) and Lucy Fisher (studio executive) made a deal to write the Louis Armstrong story, I was selected as one of the top three finalists for the writing job. I knew I increased my chances of winning the job if I came up with a great small story.

In my research, I learned a small story about Louis Armstrong and his cousin Clarence. Their relationship was incredibly interesting because Louis took care of Clarence his entire life. Everyone knew about Louis Armstrong the trumpet player, but few people knew about Louis Armstrong the compassionate man who took care of a mentally challenged family member. When it was my turn to pitch how I would write the story, I told them about Clarence. They were fascinated. My pitch was we would let Clarence narrate the biopic story of Louis Armstrong. I got the job.

In the nearly 20 years I have been writing screenplays, the small story is consistently the glue that makes the large story more interesting.

CHARACTERS

INCIDENTAL CHARACTERS

Before I get into unforgettable characters, I need to address a common error for new writers: incidental characters. These are characters who do not have anything to do with driving the story forward.

Avoid writing incidental characters. Work harder. Every character should be relevant to the story in some way. So if there is a waiter in your scene, don't give him dialogue such as, "Can I take your order please?"

Never give incidental characters dialogue. If you want your characters to leap off the page, make them interesting and part of the story. For example, make the waiter a CIA double agent with vital information.

A great example of this is written beautifully in the movie *Three Days of the Condor*. The mailman doesn't come into the scene to give mail, ask for a signature, and drive away.The mailman has a sub-machine gun and is an assassin.

This same principle applies to smaller stories such as *Nobody's Fool*. Every character who speaks in the movie has some reason to relate to Paul Newman's character, Sully. All the people at the bar or in the poker games somehow move the story along by playing important roles in Sully's life. The secretary is not just the secretary; she is also the mistress of Sully's arch rival. The awkward and annoying police officer, skillfully portrayed by Philip Seymour Hoffman, ends up pushing Sully over the edge, and Sully lands in jail.

You will occasionally see a movie or a TV show where a waiter asks, "More coffee?" or a delivery person says, "Package for Mr. Smith," but they have no other role in the story. These lines were probably not in the original script of an advanced writer. In these cases, more often than not, the producer or director wanted these incidental characters written into the script so a family member or friend can have a speaking role and get a SAG (Screen Actors Guild) card. But it never makes sense to the story, and always sticks out like a sore thumb.

Also remember that in a budget-conscious business, it makes no sense to write a speaking part for a character who doesn't need to speak and doesn't drive the story. If you do this as a writer on a TV show, you only get one or two warnings before someone taps you on the shoulder and says, "Stop adding unnecessary costs to production."

There are no incidental characters in the scripts of advanced writers. Avoid them at all costs.

UNFORGETTABLE CHARACTERS

Like death and taxes, rapt interest in characters is unavoidable. In every pitch meeting, without fail, producers and executives narrow their eyes and lean forward when I say, "Now let me tell you about a couple of the characters."

I usually stammer or stutter because I know what the lean is about. They do it subconsciously. They do it because they know this is the seminal moment for their decision to staff me on a show or buy my idea.

There will be no sale or future employment if there isn't one character your audience/executives care about, no matter how impeccable and flawless the pitch or script. Everything in your script could be perfect, but if the reader doesn't care about any of the characters, no dice.

So how do you write characters who potential buyers, employers, and audiences care about? You develop them.

DEVELOPING CHARACTERS

To develop and write characters your audience cares about, answer the following questions before you even start writing:

- What is the character's journey?

Where the character/characters begin and end is very important. No matter what race, gender, or religion the characters are, or what planet they are from, or what super-human quality they possess, if we don't care about where they start and where they end, we're not going to care about them.

If you tell the audience Superman lands on the earth, crosses the street from Starbucks, and then goes into the auto shop, no one is going to care. If you tell the audience that Flipper, the incredibly ingenious dolphin, is going to swim upstream to a quiet pool of crystal clear water, so what? Yawn. But if you say Superman is encased in an inescapable fortress of kryptonite and has to fly 100 miles into the atmosphere to stop a meteor plummeting toward earth, now we care. Or if you say Flipper has to get out of the cage and get off the boat in less than a minute to live, and then swim at mock speed to save the 10-year-old girl barely hanging onto the branch before she goes over the waterfall, the executives are going to lean forward.

Where the character begins and ends is crucial.

- What does the character want?

Like the journey, the audience has to care about what the character or characters want. If Sally wants to finish her ice cream without getting a bloated stomach, not so much. Or if Brian wants his golden retrievers to learn how to sit before nightfall, well, tell it to someone else. Conversely, if Sally wants to get out of the downtown gridlock because the doctor called and said her mother, who is suffering from Alzheimer's, only has five more minutes of lucidity, everyone cares. And if Brian can penetrate the Pentagon's defense and steal the surface-to-air missile so he can shoot down the passenger flight filled with the junior national swim team, everyone cares. Notice, even though Brian is the bad guy, we still care about what he wants. We want him to not make his goal. What the character wants is vital. And again, it has to be interesting.

- What is the personality of the protagonist or the antagonist?

Inexperienced screenwriters depict heroes as perfect characters with hurdles and obstacles in the way of the ultimate goal. Whether the goal is to save the world, a village, a family, or themselves, the heroes are written with very few imperfections. He or she must simply complete the insurmountable task at hand.

Inexperienced writers depict heroes as brave, stalwart, righteous, and God-fearing. The problem is that 99.9 percent of real heroes are tremendously flawed, cowardly, depressed, and often unfocused. Many past and present sports legends, scientists, politicians, and religious leaders have shown tremendously bad judgment. We put them on pedestals, and they constantly jump off and behave rather commonly.

I tell my students that when building heroic characters, throw as much dirt on them as possible. Make them flawed. Make their personal lives a minefield of uncertainty and vulnerability. Then take the leash off and let them try to be heroic.

Unforgiven is a great example of this theory. Clint Eastwood's character is the protagonist. He is the hero. We end up rooting for him to avenge the murder of his friend (Morgan Freeman). The character who Eastwood plays, Bill Munny, is a tarnished, reluctant hero with a villainous history. Yet, this soiled character is more true-to-life as an "every man's" protagonist.

Put the hero in a creaseless suit with perfect hair and teeth and we may keep our eyes open for a minute or two. When the hero emerges in a cesspool of pig manure, gasping for air, we sit up and wonder if he or she is going to get out of there and defuse the bomb under the Sunday school church.

Gene Hackman's character in *Unforgiven* is as mean and ruthless as an antagonist (bad guy) could ever portray. However expertly written and acted, this evil character is as dashing and charming as he is evil and heartless. This is nearly unreachable to young writers. They want to make bad characters mustache-twirling and one-dimensional— and it doesn't work.

I tell my students all the time that no matter how devious a character is, someone loves them. They must be written that way. They need to have an irresistible side. They must be as committed to their goals as their rival heroes. This is why Scarlett O'Hara is the zenith heroine all women love to hate, yet want to be. She's as flawed, ruthless, selfish, and diabolical a character as they come, yet she's vulnerable, charming, and strong. That is why we still talk about her decades later.

Real life characters operate in this gray area. Good characters are often flawed, and bad characters are often charismatic.

SPOOL OF THREAD

All characters must have that spool of thread which will ultimately reveal who they really are inside. I call it the "spool of thread" because if we find the end of the string and pull, they will unravel like a politician's plan to balance the budget. All kidding aside, all characters must have a weakness that, if revealed and exploited, would shake up their world in a cloud of dust.

13/13 AND 9/13

When developing characters for television, all character questions, answers, and rules stay the same, with an important addition. When you develop characters for television, you must know the 13/13 and the 9/13 rule.

Before pitching or writing a pilot for television, you must know which characters are the recurring characters. Traditionally, though not always the case, 13 episodes of a pilot are picked up for a trial period for ratings. The characters who will be in every single episode of your television series are known as "13/13," meaning they appear in all 13 of the 13 episodes.

There are other recurring characters who will be in most, but not all, of your episodes. These characters are only contracted for nine episodes out of 13, so they are known as your "9/13" characters. They will not appear in four episodes of every 13. Why does this happen?

As with anything, the bottom line is money. The salaries of recurring characters are a costly financial burden of a television show. The way the networks and studios cut costs is by not paying the salaries of recurring characters for four of 13 episodes.

For example, on the television show *The Unit,* we had 10 recurring characters. Only four of the 10 were contracted to be in all episodes. This meant six recurring characters were going to sit out four episodes each. Multiply these six characters by four episodes each, and a lot of money is saved for the series.

How does this affect the writers or creators of pilots? When you map out your characters, you must thoroughly develop the 13/13 characters. And when you go to pitch your television pilot, you must concentrate on these recurring characters only. You have very little time to give your pitch, so it pays to leave the 9/13 characters out of your pitch.

EXAMPLES OF GREAT CHARACTERS

To really get to know how to develop great characters, read scripts or watch movies and TV shows with compelling characters. Who are your favorite characters and why? Here is a short list of some of mine (and why). Use the lessons from what you observe about your favorite characters (and mine) to develop your own compelling characters.

Note: The following characters are movie characters. There are as many or more legendary three dimensional television characters that will live on in my mind such as Tony Soprano, Detective Vic Mackey, Dexter Morgan, Dr. Gregory House, Walter H. White, Omar Little, Jackie Payton, Nancy Botwin, and many, many other extraordinary characters played by extraordinary actors and actresses. For the sake of exercise the following examples are movie characters.

PROTAGONISTS (HEROES)

Tender Mercies (1983)
– Mac Sledge, played by Robert Duvall and written by Horton Foote. This is the movie I attribute to wanting to become a screenwriter. The movie was brilliantly written. The protagonist was symbolic of the kind of protagonist I was inspired to write. Mac Sledge was flawed and barely redeemable, and his triumphs never towered above his vulnerabilities. This character is perfectly human.

Glory (1989)
– Private Trip, played by Denzel Washington and written by Robert Gould Shaw, Kevin Jarre, and Lincoln Kirstein. How could writers have the courage to write a character who was a self-centered, self-serving slave? Private Trip is annoying and heroic, much like most historical leaders of all countries.

Unforgiven (1992)
– Bill Munny, played by Clint Eastwood and written by David Webb Peoples. I never write or teach a class without using this movie as a model of the perfect script. Bill Munny is the most despicable hero ever portrayed. This character is truly three-dimensional.

What's Love Got to Do With It (1993)
– Tina Turner, played by Angela Bassett and written by Tina Turner and Kurt Loder. Most abused men and women find a "why" to venture back to the abuse. There is nothing heroic in martyrdom. Somehow this character rises from the ashes to become a true phoenix.

True Romance (1993)
– Alabama Whitman, played by Patricia Arquette and written by Quentin Tarantino. Alabama is a female prostitute who has a quiet voice, but fights like a lion. She steals, murders, makes all the wrong choices, and we still cheer for her. Perfect writing.

Nobody's Fool (1995)
– Sully Sullivan, played by Paul Newman and written by Richard Russo and Robert Benton. Sometimes it's hard to look past Paul Newman's masterful performance. Sully Sullivan is a character who is selfish, cowardly, and mean-spirited, with a chip on his shoulder the size of a small country. Nonetheless, we can't help but love the guy. This is one of the smallest and yet most gigantic scripts of all time. The same must be said about Paul Newman's performance.

Hustle & Flow (2005)
– Nola played by Taryn Manning and written by Craig Brewer. A dopey prostitute who can't seem to think her way out of a paper bag becomes Joan of Arc, and you barely notice. This is a great example of a flawed, three-dimensional character. We shouldn't want to cheer for her, but we do.

ANTAGONISTS (VILLIANS)

Once Upon a Time in the West (1968)
– Cheyenne, played by Jason Robards and written by Dario Argento and Bernardo Bertolucci. When I was a young kid and we played the characters of this movie over and over, I always wanted to be Cheyenne. Not until I was much older

did I realize Cheyenne was a ruthless killer and leader of a band of outlaws. This character seems to be the most thoughtful character in this violent epic.

At Close Range (1986)
– Brad Whitewood Sr., played by Christopher Walken and written by Elliot Lewett and Nicolas Kazan. I was living in Manhattan, New York. I was bored and decided to slip into a theater to watch a movie I had never heard about. I left the theater shaking like a dry leaf in the wind. This movie deeply disturbed me. I sat there, riveted on Christopher Walken and his charm and likeability. At the end of the film, he was the devil himself. This is how to write a villain. Make them charming, lovable, admirable—and then let them murder brutally beyond belief.

Street Smart (1987)
– Fast Black, played by Morgan Freeman and written by David Freeman. This character was written (as well as portrayed) with razor blade elegance. The character of Fast Black was one of the first times I remember thinking how alluring it was to be a criminal.

Unforgiven (1992)
– Little Bill Daggett played by Gene Hackman and written by David Webb Peoples. There was something so sensible and reasonable about Little Bill Daggett, but he was human nitroglycerin. I still don't know if Little Bill or Bill Munny was the hero or the villain. This is exactly how most sports, spiritual, and political heroes are today. Good people dressed in lamb's clothes, with the decency of wolves.

True Romance (1993)
– Drexel Spivey, played by Gary Oldman and written by

Quentin Tarantino. (No one writes bad guys with as much likeability as Quentin Tarantino.) Drexel Spivey is a true demon, but his lines are still quotable and fun.

Out of Sight (1998)
– Maurice Miller, played by Don Cheadle and written by Elmore Leonard and Scott Frank. This character should be totally unlikeable, but somehow he isn't. His complete lack of conscience is offset by his laid-back cool demeanor and understated humor. We don't necessarily root for him, but we do like to watch him.

3:10 to Yuma (2007)
– Ben Wade played by Russell Crowe and written by Halsted Welles and Michael Brandt. The problem with hating Ben Wade is that he isn't a one-faced devil. Throughout the story we are shown his humanity in small but significant ways. How can we find such a ruthless, cold-blooded killer charming and even somewhat redeemable? Because the writers carefully crafted him that way, and because Crowe's acting was spot on.

X-Men First Class (2011)
– Erik Lehnsherr, played by Michael Fassbender, written by Ashley Miller, Zack Stentz, Jane Goldman, and Matthew Vaughn.This comic book, superhero movie, was written, directed and performed with excellence on par with any Academy Award winning movie. The Character Erik Lehnsherr was not portrayed as a one-note villain who the viewers could dismiss. Instead, we were drawn under his skin to develop the same amount of rage and contempt as the antagonist. Hats off to the writers for taking the audience on a journey inside the mind a likable mutant to a villain who justifiably wants to destroy mankind. Hooray for bad guys!

A SCENE

If you can write and construct a scene, you can write a feature film or a television pilot. The problem is, most people don't know how to write a scene.

This is good for me because I make most of my money doing re-writes. The first thing I do when I read a screenplay I have been hired to re-write is to go through the entire script to see how many actual scenes already exist. Most of the time there are no more than ten true scenes in a script that requires many more—thus, the need for a re-write. Perhaps the last thing I should do is shout from the mountaintops, "This is how you write a scene!"

This would serve me, but not my students. So to help my students become the best writers they can possibly be, I'm going to share the correct way to write a scene.

WHAT IS A SCENE?

A scene is when a character has a pressing, immediate need to achieve something (such as love, power, survival, revenge, or understanding)—the reason he or she showed up in the scene. The character's attempt to get this immediate, pressing need met will result in failure. This failure tells us the scene is over. This failure will also always force the character to rethink how to achieve his or her goal.

More simply, a scene is when a character wants something immediately, and the failure to get what he or she wants propels us to the next scene. The collection of all these failures over the course of the story is the plot.

The character's failure to achieve his or her immediate need must inspire the reader to know what happens next. If the reader (producer, director, and actor) doesn't want to know what happens next, then the scene has failed. After all, if the script reader isn't interested (bored, snoozing, yawning), the viewing audience watching the film or TV show won't be interested either, and nobody wants a failed project.

A classic example of a real scene is portrayed over and over in formulaic themes in action movies like *Predator* and *The Terminator*. The scene begins with an unstoppable force mowing down men, women, and children, and leaving death and destruction in its wake.

Our protagonist (hero) finds a weapon, like a gun, picks it up, aims, and fires several rounds into the unstoppable force. The bullets have no effect on the unstoppable force, which keeps coming. End of scene.

The next scene begins when the unstoppable force mows down yet more men, women, and children, leaving more death and destruction in its wake. Our protagonist picks up a flame-thrower and turns it on the unstoppable force, but the fire has no effect on the unstoppable force that keeps coming. End of scene.

Remember the pressing, immediate need is to survive the unstoppable force. The minute something stops the unstoppable force, the movie is over.

CREATE A REAL, COMPELLING SCENE

To write interesting stories that are compelling, can be sold, and also represent you as the writer, you must write real scenes. They must be page-turning, without a lull until the last page. This gives you a chance to become a paid screenwriter.

CREATE STAND-ALONE SCENES

To write a real scene, keep in mind all scenes also must stand alone. This means the audience does not need to know what happened in the scene before or after the scene to understand the present scene. Many writers say, "But I have to get my character across town to see her mother, so she has to go on a long bus ride." This is not a scene. Two people holding hands singing Kumbaya as they skip to the ice cream store is not a scene.

If the character needs to get across town to save her mother's life, and the bus that arrives blows up, that is a scene. It stands alone; it propels the character to have to do something different. That is also the end of the scene. If the two people holding hands, singing Kumbaya as they skip to the ice cream store, find everyone in the ice cream store dead, that is a scene. It propels us to wonder what happens next.

Students and professional writers argue until they are blue in the face. Everyone points out examples in television shows and films where there is no pressing need. Forget what happens after the script is written. There are too many things that happen from the page to the director, actors, and editors to explain why the end result on film has no pressing need and the character doesn't fail. Forget all that. Writers must only concentrate on their pages and on the pressing needs.

THE EXCEPTION TO THE RULE

The exception to the rule is a SURPRISE.

When a character doesn't want anything immediately or doesn't have an immediate, pressing need for power, love, survival, revenge, or understanding, there can be a surprise.

For example, a woman can be walking down the street happy as a lark. This character stops to pick up a foreign object, only to find out the object is ticking. The object is ticking because it is a bomb. This is now a scene because there is a pressing, immediate need—the need to escape being blown to smithereens.

When a character is having a boring conversation with another character about the weather, and then someone bolts into the room with a suitcase full of money and a gun and says, "Hold this, I will be back after the killers arrive"—now we have an immediate and pressing need. Will the characters choose to keep the gun and money, or run? The characters now have to take immediate action.

I often use the television original series *24* as the best example of how to write scenes. There is always a pressing need, and the result is failure that propels the characters, the story, and the viewing audience into the next scene. You can't go to the refrigerator during any part of *24* or you will miss something important. The intrigue and excitement never lets up. Do yourself a favor if you have never seen the show and rent or buy the DVD's.

I was writing on a television show and the writers were all trying to crank out an episode. I raised my hand and told the executive producer the scene we just wrote was not a scene. Nothing happened; there was no pressing need to achieve, and there was no failure.

The executive producer gave me the one-eye and said, "I know nothing happens, but it's cute, so leave it." When we started to shoot the episode, guess which scene was the first to be cut by the director? Yes, the cute scene was the first to go. The director was on a time crunch, and over budget. This scene did not advance the story, so was not needed.

Never write scenes that do not advance the story. If it's boring on the page, it will be boring on the screen, and therefore skipped. When a producer or director skips too many scenes, the script is tossed in the trash, and the writer isn't hired again.

A long time ago, there was a screenplay that sold for a record amount of money. Everyone in Hollywood wanted to read the script, which was written by the immensely talented writer Shane Black. I had not read the script, even though it was the talk of the town. Every jealous screenwriter shot holes in the script, to the point where I lost interest in reading it. Finally, I got a hold of a shooting copy. I sat down and read the script in a record amount of time because I could not turn the pages fast enough. When I came to the last page, I thought, "This script is worth every penny spent on it." The script was flawless. There was nothing cute or remotely boring about it. I, too, was jealous. The truth is, you can write like Shane Black if you write page-turning scenes where readers are excited to know what happens next.

A GOOD SCENE VS. A COMPELLING SCENE

Let's examine the following scene to see if it qualifies as a true scene (INT means INTERIOR, EXT means EXTERIOR, and POV means POINT OF VIEW).

INT. POLICE DIVISION 7 – DAY

Chara enters the station, dressed in her hospital greens. Her uniform is in dry cleaner plastic over her shoulders. She turns toward a commotion.

POV: The Gang Task Force Detective has a young, tattooed, African-American male handcuffed—shoves him through the division.

The Gang Task Force Detective sees—

POV: Chara as she surveys the situation.

The Gang Task Force Detective hands the young male off to be booked, then turns to walk toward Chara.

GANG DETECTIVE

Officer—

CHARA

Yeah—

The Gang Task Force Detective looks her up and down.

GANG DETECTIVE

You're a reserve—?

> CHARA

How'd you know?

> GANG DETECTIVE

(points to her name tag)

'Trauma Center Surgeon' is a great undercover, right?

Chara looks at her name tag—blushes.

> CHARA

Who was the kid—?

> GANG DETECTIVE

'Lil' JoJo—we have no wits, other than your statement, which would never hold up in court.

> CHARA

How'd you pick him up?

GANG DETECTIVE

Got him with the gun, matching powder
burns—even got his finger prints.

(and then)

You did good. We had nothing to go on,
but you gave us the name.

Chara nods, unsatisfied.

The scene is interesting. It actually qualifies as a
standalone scene. We don't need a scene before it or after it
to explain what is going on. Chara is a Reserve Officer
reporting for duty and a Gang Task Force Officer stops her to
inform her that they picked up a suspect on her lead.

Did Chara or the Gang Force Officer want something
or have a pressing need to achieve something and fail? I say
no. No one showed up in the scene with a pressing need and
failed; we do not need to turn the page and ask what
happens next.

Is there a surprise? Mildly, but nothing earth-
shattering. Chara is dressed like a doctor, but turns out to be
a Reserve Officer. Yawn.

Now let's examine another scene from the same
script.

INT. PATROL CAR – DAY

OFFICER MARY KELLY, early-30's, second generation Irish, attractive, two ROCKERS above a DIAMOND patch on her shoulder, rides along with OFFICER CHARA ROMERO, mid-30's, hispanic, girl-next-door pretty, no BARS, no ROCKERS on her shoulder—

They ride in silence. They both scan the streets when they both spot—

POV: A SUSPECT, male Caucasian, late-30's, jeans, white T-shirt, sneakers, leans into the back seat of a car.

Chara points—

> MARY

>> I see it—

Mary picks up the microphone of the MDT—calls it in.

> MARY

>> 7 Adam 23—possible GTA in progress. Requesting back up and air unit—

RADIO

Copy 7 Adam 23—what is your location?

MARY

Anchorage and Third on a white male.

RADIO

Copy Anchorage and Third—an air unit
is on its way.

MARY

Copy.

Mary navigates to the curb—

EXT. STREET

The Suspect doesn't see or hear Mary and Chara get out of
the patrol car. They both slide their batons through their
baton rings.

> MARY
>
> (commanding)
>
> Excuse me, Sir—back away from the vehicle, please.

Mary comes around the driver's side of the patrol car; Chara creeps toward the outside of the passenger door. They've flanked the Suspect.

The Suspect is caught completely off guard. Backs out of the car, turns toward Mary and Chara.

> SUSPECT
>
> This is my girlfriend's car, she can't find her keys.

> MARY
>
> (more forceful)
>
> Sir, face away, on your knees, palms in the air, now—

The Suspect ignores the command—inches toward them.

SUSPECT

I told you it's my girlfriend's car—

Mary unhooks her holster, removes her gun, LOW READY position. Chara mirrors her partner—both weapons, low ready.

CHARA

(shouts)

Face away—prone now, palms up—

SUSPECT

Hey, hold on a minute—

Mary and Chara move their guns to READY position.

The Suspect reaches behind his back—

Mary and Chara raise their guns to ON TARGET position.

The Suspect starts to pull something from around his back—

POV: The Suspect wheels a HANDGUN around, points at Chara—

Mary FIRES TWO SHOTS—

POV: The Suspect FLIES back, hits the ground, shoulders first.

Mary and Chara approach with caution, guns still ON TARGET. Chara gets to the Suspect first, looks up to make sure—

POV: Mary still has her gun on the Suspect.

Chara cuffs the Suspect.

Mary secures the area with a sweeping glance, keys her Rover on, speaks into her microphone.

                    MARY
        Officer needs help—shots fired.

Chara checks the Suspect's vitals; looks around, removes her cell phone, punches the keys.

CHARA

This is Chara Romero—I need you to set up the OR room in less than twenty minutes. I've got a GSW to the abdomen and he's bleeding briskly, conscious and breathing. I believe the on-call surgeon is Chris Chiles. His number is 555-1313; notify him immediately.

Chara hangs up her cell phone—checks the Suspect's pulse.

This scene is written much better. It stands alone. We don't need a scene before or after to explain what is going on.

Is there a pressing need for Chara and Mary to show up in the scene? Absolutely. They want to know whether or not a crime is being committed; indeed, there is. Do they succeed in stopping the crime? Yes, but not in the way they wanted. They did not apprehend the suspect without shooting, which is considered a failure in every Police Manual in America.

At the end of the scene, Chara calls in the OIS (Officer Involved Shooting), but she appears to be an expert at dealing with the hospital beyond her job as a Reserve Police Officer. Do we want to know what happens next? Yes. Does the suspect die? Will Chara and Mary suffer consequences for shooting a suspect? And who is Chara? Why does she know so much about hospital procedure?

Note: It is not written whether these two scenes come from a television episode or a feature film. We don't need to know. All we need to know is how to write a scene, and the reader or audience wants to know what happens next.

SCENES WITH GUEST STARS – IT'S NOT THEIR SHOW

Unfortunately for aspiring screenwriters, there are a few things you usually don't learn unless you are hired to write a movie or you are staffed on a television show (or unless you read my book). For example, most classes don't teach you how to write a bottle or submarine episode so your line producer will love you, or how to professionally offer a film producer a "producer's draft" without getting in trouble with your agent or union.

One of the things that is also hard to learn without actually working on a television show is how to write scenes involving guest stars. It sounds as if it would be simple, but it isn't.

Two bank robbers (guest stars) steal the money, drive away, go into a motel, spread the money all over the bed, and take turns doing back flips into the cash. So, what is wrong with this scenario? If you write a scene like this more than twice, you may get fired from your writing job paying you $10,000 a week.

In the writers' room one of my favorite executive producers used to chide me and say, "Sterling, it is not the guest star's show."

I guarantee you that my favorite executive producer only had to chide me once. Although she said it in jest, she was trying to protect me from not delivering what the network wanted. Do not deliver what the network wants and the network will not want you anymore.

So, whenever you write a scene for a television show, you better include one of your principal stars, the 13/13 or the 9/13. When young writers construct beautifully crafted, dramatic scenes, and the studio and network pay hundreds of thousands of dollars for the director to shoot footage, that footage better include one of those really expensive regulars on the show. Hundreds of thousands of dollars to feature two guest stars (day players) who will not return on the show is not good for ratings or job security.

For example, in a comedy show like *Two and a Half Men*, where the four or five principals make a gag of money per episode, one of those principals must be in the scene or else the writers will not write for that show for long.

Besides cost, there is another reason for including a principal in each scene that features a guest star. If a guest star has a serious point of view in the story other than to be killed, you can bet that guest star will be featured for more than one episode. Why?

Because it is not the guest star's show.

Guest stars must interact with one of the principal characters because it is the principal character's show. That is why principal characters get paid a king's ransom to come back every week and do it again. Guest stars receive a week's pay and go on to hopefully be a guest star on another show or, God willing, they may one day become stars of their own show. Either way, writers beware—guest stars don't get their own scenes.

DIALOGUE

FADE IN:

ON A LIGHT BOX—

Sits a number of CAT SCAN X-RAYS, which are ghostly, bilateral, black and white monochrome depictions.

> DR. JAMISON
>
> Spring would be miraculous. With a handful of four-leaf clovers, I'd say April.

INT. NEW YORK – DOCTOR STEPHEN JAMISON'S OFFICE – DAY

PULL BACK TO REVEAL—

Wood paneled walls, books, and medical journals vie for space; medical certificates hang with aplomb on the walls.

AND FURTHER BACK—

DOCTOR STEPHEN JAMISON, early-50's, white hospital frock over nice shirt, tie, slacks, sits at his desk, looks up—

POV: Sitting opposite Dr. Jamison is CHARLES HAMLYN, 44, medium height and on the thin side, pepper gray hair cropped short, pale fierce eyes. He wears a custom-tailored suit, gun-metal gray.

Charles is locked in a THOUSAND-YARD STARE out the WINDOW. He only folds his hands and presses the tips of his fingers against his lips. He has an unlikeable expression that he's learned to perfect—

> DR. JAMISON
>
> I wish there was a way to pay someone to do this for you—

Charles doesn't BLINK or respond.

> DR. JAMISON
>
> Charles—

CHARLES

(almost to himself)

I had a great workout today.

(and then)

I can still do a push up for every year I've
been alive.

DR. JAMISON

That's something to be happy about.

The scene above is between a doctor and his patient.
Nowhere in the dialogue does the doctor tell his patient that
the patient only has three months to live. Also, nowhere in
the dialogue does the patient tell the doctor that the patient
is disappointed. Why?

Dialogue is not meant to tell the story.

The last thing screenwriters seem to master is
dialogue. To begin with, most writers feel dialogue should be
the narrative that explains what is going on. The opposite is
true. Dialogue should be the *last* thing given to a script.

A SILENT MOVIE

A great mentor, David Mamet, once told me all scripts should be written as a silent movie. This wisdom forces the writer to not tell the story, but show the story.

SHOW DON'T TELL

Showing, not telling, separates novice writers from experienced writers. We should never use dialogue to make Walker (the character) explain to us how much rage he feels. Instead, use action to bring Walker into the room, pick up an ashtray, and hurl it into the china cabinet. Now it is apparent that Walker feels rage, even though he hasn't said a word.

It should be said to screenwriters, a thousand times a day, "Show, don't tell."

FLAT LINE DIALOGUE

So many of us make the mistake of having all our characters sound alike. If we (the writers) are quick-witted with snappy dialogue, all our characters are quick-witted and snappy. If we are slow to the punch, thoughtful, sparse with words, so are our characters.

SYNCOPATION AND PENTAMETER

The Oxford Dictionary describes syncopation as: "To displace the beats or accents in a passage so that strong beats become weak and vice versa."

The Oxford Dictionary describes pentameter as: "A form of Greek or Latin dactylic verse composed of two halves each of two feet and a long syllable, used to elegiac verse." (Say that three times as fast as you can with your eyes closed, while standing on one leg.)

My definitions are less scholarly. I tell my students to vary the words from character to character (syncopate), and vary the meter (pentameter) at which your characters speak.

Not every character can be smart and amble with one-liners, or be slow, pensive, and thoughtful like Sam Sheppard starring in a Sam Sheppard play. When characters are all funny, fast, slow, or pedantic, it flatlines the dialogue. It's boring and not believable. Mix up the pace, accents, slang, and diction of all characters to avoid writing flat dialogue.

The cleverness of syncopation and pentameter can let us know all we need sometimes. When Sally asks Jayd, "What is wrong?" and Jayd replies, "Nothing," we may never understand that something is indeed wrong. But when Sally asks Jayd, "What is wrong?" and Jayd replies (too quickly), "Nothing," the rapid speed (pentameter) of his response lets us know something is, indeed, very wrong.

The use of no response to a question can also tell us what we need to know. If Mary asks Bill, "Would you like a kiss?" and Bill responds, "Oh, sure," we're not convinced that Bill really wants that kiss. However, when Mary asks Bill, "Would you like a kiss?" and Bill says nothing, but a slow smile spreads across his lips (syncopate), we all know what Bill wants.

The rhythm and speed of the above questions gives us a richer tone and appreciation for the script. This is why syncopation and pentameter are so important in writing scripts.

WHY WAS LANGUAGE INVENTED?

The most important lesson I share with my students is often the most surprising: dialogue is not meant to help the characters to communicate. It is the exact opposite: Dialogue is meant to keep people from knowing what's on our minds.

It's worth repeating. Language (dialogue) was invented to keep other people from knowing what we are thinking.

Think about it. When a man walks into a restaurant and sees a lone, curvaceous woman sitting at the bar, he doesn't saunter up to her, look her up and down, and then ask her if she would like to go have sex. That's what he's thinking, but that's not what he says. We men are far more deceptive than that. We saunter up to a woman and we tell her that she has a nice purse. The woman may act flattered, but she knows there is no man on the planet who gives a damn about a purse. She knows the man is trying to lure her into the net. Great actors can look at a line like "nice purse" and deliver it in such a way that there is no mistaking the real intent.

For another example, consider this: A woman flies into the market to pick up a few last minute items. She has no makeup and her hair is in curlers under a scarf, but she believes she can do it without running into anyone she knows. When she does run into the one person she never wanted to see under this circumstance, she doesn't let fly with, "Damn, can't I just get something quickly without running into you?" Not a chance. This woman under curlers and duress will flash a smile and say, "Wonderful day, isn't it?"

Language is most commonly used to manipulate and deceive. Remember this, and use it when you write dialogue.

When I was a teenager, my mother would stop me from leaving the house with an insult from left field, such as, "You're not going to wear that shirt are you? That shirt looks hideous."

Her words did the trick, and stopped me in my tracks, which is exactly what she wanted to do. Then she would quickly come up with something for me to do.

What my mother really wanted was for me not to run down the street to cohort with the neighborhood bimbo. She was too manipulative and deceptive to say she didn't want me to go see the neighborhood bimbo. She knew those words would only enforce my rebellion and make that girl become the neighborhood superhero to me. But telling me my shirt "looks hideous" attacked me on all cylinders. My appearance was much more important than my mother's opinion of the neighborhood bimbo. She knew it, and used words to disguise her true intent.

When a man cannot deliver the sexual goods on a particular evening, the last thing a woman responds with is, "Man, you really missed out because I was going to give you the thrill of your life. Guess I should call the other guy I was thinking about." That is never what the woman says. What she says is, "That's okay, honey, let's just cuddle."

In review, dialogue should be the last thing that goes into a script. All scripts should be written, as much as possible, like a silent movie. Show, don't tell. Dialogue should be added when there is no other choice.

When we do add dialogue, it should be to deceive and manipulate, not to communicate. No man barges into the house to tell his wife, "Sex has to happen by the time I get my tie off." The wife would show the husband where the cot in the garage is located. Instead, the husband bolts through the door and sheepishly asks, "Are you busy?" while he suggestively caresses the small of her back.

STRUCTURE IN FILM SCRIPTS

Structure in television and film writing is ever-changing. Writers must keep up with the changes because if the structure is dated, the readers view the scripts as dated and amateur.

FEATURE FILMS

The old paradigm was that feature films were supposed to be between 115 to 120 pages. The general breakdown was:

Old:

Pages 1–10: The setup and start of Act One

Pages 25–35: The end of Act One (somewhere in this vicinity)

Pages 30–90: Act Two (starting at page 30 – 35 on average)

Pages 90–110: Act Three

Pages 110–120: Resolution

This paradigm was followed for years, and is still in some books and classrooms. This is a shame, because the new paradigm is that feature scripts should be less than 100 pages.

Several years ago, I remember when Richard LaGravenses turned in the draft of *Bridges of Madison County*. It was a staggeringly short 95 pages. I remember the memos that went around the studios. It was something akin to "Great read, but he didn't finish." At the time, few people had seen a finished script less than a 100 pages. A director came on board and immediately released his hounds to rewrite Richard's script. Fortunately, the rewrites didn't pan out. Clint Eastwood was brought in to direct, and Richard's script was eventually shot.

Now, this is the norm. Most directors bring in their own writers, and feature scripts are now less than 100 pages. For my last three feature film writing assignments, the producers and studio executives all instructed me to keep the final draft less than 100 pages.

So mathematically, how does the new paradigm, 95 pages, affect the old structure? Now that the scripts are 25 and 30 pages leaner, the setup, first, second, third act break, and resolution have to be shifted toward the front of the screenplay. The major reconstruction comes in the second act. Here's how it (roughly) plays out:

New:

Pages 1–10: The setup and start of Act One (basically the same, but you MUST capture attention in the first five pages to get anyone to keep reading)

Page 25: The end of Act One (somewhere in this vicinity)

Pages 25–65: Act Two (ending at page 65 on average)

Pages 65–85: Act Three

Pages 85–95: Resolution

To step back and look at this, it seems to make sense. There is only one problem: Most readers in networks, agencies, production companies, and studios never read more than 10 pages if the script does not grab them. This is the flat truth—no one reads past page 10 if they are not hooked. I have first-hand experience. I have dated my share of development executives (the seekers of the next great scripts), and my eyes were involuntarily opened to the way this works.

Development executive date and I would sit on the couch together, each doing our work. I would write or just stare at the computer and beg it to write for me. My date had a stack of scripts from floor to ceiling. She would read a few pages, and then toss the script. She'd read another script and toss it. Whenever she got out her pen to mark on the page of a script, I knew the script had made the cut. Every so often the pen or marker would come out and she'd attack the page like an inspired abstract painter; during these few times, I felt proud for the writer.

The thing is, script readers and development executives have to take home 15 to 20 scripts a night and report back to their bosses. These screenplays include movies in development, which means writers they have already hired wrote the scripts. The other scripts are solicitations as potential scripts for the networks or studios to purchase.

Now here is the key—"the kicker," as the saying goes. No one can possibly read 20 scripts a night. If you put a stop watch next to me and say "Go," the fastest I can read one script is 90 minutes. This means 20 scripts would take me 30 hours to complete.

So how does a development executive manage to read 15 to 20 scripts a night? The answer is, she doesn't. The fact is, development executives read five pages of a script and if they are not gripped by then, they toss the script over their shoulders and go on to the next one. This is an absolute fact. I have seen it time and time again.

What does this mean?

It means no script has 10 pages to get the setup down. The setup and the first big grab should be by page two and no longer than page five. To repeat, if you're trying to sell a script, you have to do it by page five. No one in town reads more than 10 pages. I guarantee, if you haven't got them by page five, they will not read on through to page 10.

SPINS AND TURNS

A "spin" or "turn" is when the story is going in one direction, then suddenly takes a right angle or 180 degree turn and goes in another direction. Spins and turns keep the audience in their seats, inside of getting up to get popcorn or use the bathroom. It also keeps the attention of the producer or development executive who has 20 other scripts to read that evening.

If your script is going to grab attention, it better have some surprises (spins and turns), which typically appear as transitions from one act to the other. The story might lead the reader/audience to think it is going in a predictable direction, when—surprise!—it presents an unexpected twist. Wow! Didn't expect *that*! This is what keeps them reading.

If you want your story to be interesting, captivating, and SOLD, you increase your chances by presenting effective spins and turns.

PUTTING IT ALL TOGETHER

Okay, so to ensure the concept of "grab 'em by page five" and "include spins and turns" is not lost in conceptual translation, let's make up a feature film story:

(Of course there will be a few holes and inconsistencies because we're only making it up. We are not getting paid to flush the following story out and make it perfect. This is only an exercise.)

THE WEARY DETECTIVE

Our story, *The Weary Detective,* is about a troubled detective who has lost the feeling for being a cop. He's riding out his last couple years and wants nothing "hot" to come across his desk while he's on rotation (his shift).

Our detective has marital problems, and his teenage daughter is estranged, to say the least. All those years of hard charging up the ranks from the police academy to making detective second grade has taken a toll on his marriage and his relationship with his rebellious teen. He was never home. Now he wants to be home. He wants his wife to look at him again with love and lust in her eyes. He wants his daughter to stop looking like the Goth, emo, night of the living dead.

One night he catches a murder case. No problem. Most murders can be solved quickly because they happen so close to home. Family disputes gone wrong. A jealous boyfriend or girlfriend lost it and hits someone over the head with a bat.

Now the heat our detective wanted no part of comes across his desk. The dead body is linked to a serial killer the FBI has been tracking for months. Now our detective sees interaction with the Feebees (FBI), which he hates. And all eyes are going to be on him and his open case. Our detective sees long hours and no chance to spend some time with his wife, or remotely get to know his dark teenager.

He goes to his Watch Commander to see if he can take a pass on the murder case. The Watch Commander says, "No way." (These two men have a shaky relationship. One gives orders, the other does whatever he can to never follow them.)

The first spin, or turn, in the investigation comes when the murder case ends up being an FBI serial killer case.

ADDING MORE SPINS OR TURNS

When the FBI puts the suspect's file on our detective's desk, and he discovers the prime suspect is his brother-in-law, Mike (the husband of his wife's sister, and his daughter's favorite uncle), we now have our second spin or turn. Things have just gotten much more interesting.

Now our detective's problems are adding up at a rapid pace. He has a hot case. He has to deal with the FBI. He has to spend more time away from a crumbling marriage. And now he must throw a grenade on his marriage and relationship with his daughter by telling his wife and estranged daughter that Uncle Mike is the prime murder suspect.

Our detective decides to keep everything close to his chest until some questions are answered. He pays a visit to his brother-in-law, only to find a woman in his company at the wrong place at the wrong time. Our detective discovers his brother-in-law is having an affair (a new spin). Now things have really deteriorated. His brother-in-law is not only a serial killer suspect; he is also cheating on the sister of our detective's wife.

The detective now has to decide whether to keep everything even closer to his chest, or risk a family disaster by telling his wife and daughter that Uncle Mike is no good. Obstacles, obstacles, and more obstacles are the solid framework of good drama.

The detective makes a nice dinner for his wife and daughter. They all sit down to a candlelight dinner, and the detective tells them about his case—and that Uncle Mike is the prime suspect. The wife tells him this is the end of the line. She wants to separate, and the daughter swears to never speak to him again. They storm off to leave the detective with three cold plates.

The Watch Commander calls the detective into his office to tell him that he's going to be pulled off the case. The detective now realizes the only thing he might have is the case. As he fights with the Watch Commander, the detective receives a call from the hospital. His daughter has overdosed (yet another spin).

The detective needs to rally with his wife to pull their daughter out of her doldrums. Husband and wife must postpone their inevitable train wreck to save their daughter.

A call comes from the detective's partner asking him to come back from the hospital and look at some surprising evidence the FBI overlooked. The detective must once again choose between family and career. He opts to stay at the hospital, possibly putting another wedge between himself and his supervisor.

The partner pleads with the detective to hear him out. There is evidence that absolves the detective's brother-in-law. It seems Uncle Mike has an air-tight alibi. They are back to square one. Both families are wounded beyond repair.

The detective returns from the hospital and gets an unexpected visitor to the police division. A teenage boy shows up and tells the detective that he (the teenager) is the boyfriend of the detective's daughter. He says he and the daughter are harboring a secret. The daughter is pregnant (another spin).

This is the moment in feature films where they will call everything a losing proposition—the moment the protagonist realizes he or she can't win. This is the house burned down, the dog has been run over, and the wife has gone over a cliff moment. There must be a moment in every good feature film, whether drama or comedy, where the protagonist cannot win—where the "spool of thread" starts to unravel. The coffin is nailed shut and there is no light of day. The protagonist needs a miracle or *deus ex machina* moment. Our protagonist's life has come apart at the seams.

Now we insert an overlooked piece of evidence that gives a tiny spark. It may come when the protagonist goes to try to patch up things with his daughter. The daughter may say something that makes the protagonist remember something he tossed away. Now he remembers that the mistress of the brother-in-law, Uncle Mike, made a strange comment. Our protagonist follows his instinct and finds the missing element that ties the brother-in-law's mistress to the string of murders.

Her arrest is a false ending because the audience knows the protagonist has to still climb Mount Everest to have a needle in the haystack chance of repairing his personal life.

The solid framework of good drama? Obstacles, obstacles, and more obstacles (spins and turns). Okay, so now that we have an interesting story with plenty of spins and turns, let's put this story together structurally.

OUR FEATURE FILM STRUCTURALLY

SETUP/ACT ONE

Our troubled detective is riding out his last couple years. He has marital problems, and his teenage daughter is estranged. One night he catches a murder case. No problem. Most murders can be solved quickly. But this one is different—it is the heat our detective wanted no part of anymore.

(SPIN)

The dead body is linked to a serial killer the FBI has been tracking for months. High profile. This will interfere with his "back to family" goals.

PAGE 5

Seeing long hours and no chance to spend some time with his wife, or remotely get to know his dark teenager, the detective goes to his Watch Commander to see if he can take a rain check. Watch Commander says, "No way."

PAGE 10

(SPIN)

The detective discovers the prime suspect is his brother-in-law, Mike (the husband of his wife's sister, and his daughter's favorite uncle).

Because this new information will harm his already crumbling family life, our detective decides to keep everything close to his chest until some questions are answered.

(SPIN)

The detective pays a visit to his brother-in-law and finds out his brother-in-law is having an affair. He even has a few words with the mistress. Now things have really deteriorated and he doesn't know what to do.

PAGE 25: END OF ACT ONE

ACT TWO

The detective makes a nice dinner for his wife and daughter, where the detective tells them about his case and that Uncle Mike is the prime suspect. The two women get mad and storm off to leave the detective with three cold plates.

The Watch Commander calls the detective into his office to tell him that he's going to be pulled off the case. The detective now realizes the only thing he might have is the case, so he argues with the Watch Commander to keep the case (which confuses the Watch Commander since the detective initially wanted to be removed from the case).

The Watch Commander looks into the detective's eyes and notices the detective is in pain. The case is exactly what the detective needs to keep his mind off his troubles. The Watch Commander reinstates the detective, who receives a call from the hospital.

(SPIN)

His daughter has overdosed.

PAGE 45: MIDDLE OF ACT TWO

The detective and his wife must postpone their inevitable train wreck to save their daughter.

While at the hospital, the detective's partner calls about surprising evidence the FBI has overlooked. The detective opts to stay at the hospital with his family, risking his job.

(SPIN)

The partner reveals evidence that absolves the detective's brother-in-law. Uncle Mike has an air-tight alibi. They are back to square one, but the family is wounded beyond repair.

(SPIN)

The detective gets an unexpected visitor to the police division. A teenage boy shows up and announces he is the boyfriend of the detective's daughter. He tells the detective that he and the detective's daughter are harboring a secret. The daughter is pregnant.

The detective is now in a losing proposition. The spool of thread unravels.

PAGE 65: END OF ACT TWO

ACT THREE

(SPIN)

Now we insert an overlooked piece of evidence that gives a tiny spark. When the protagonist goes to try to patch up things with his daughter, she (the daughter) says something that makes the protagonist remember something he tossed away. Now he remembers the mistress of the brother-in-law made a strange comment that may be tied to the case.

Our protagonist follows his instinct and finds the missing element that ties the brother-in-law's mistress to a string of murders.

PAGE 85: END OF ACT THREE

RESOLUTION

The arrest of the mistress is a false ending because the audience knows the protagonist has a long way to go to repair his personal life.

The Watch Commander calls the detective into his office to congratulate him, and to offer a peace treaty and a promotion. Our detective tells the Watch Commander to "Take this job and shove it."

Our detective goes back to his family to make amends.

PAGE 95: END OF MOVIE

The old paradigm subscribed to three spins. Our made up story has how many spins? Many more than three. Yes, the more spins the better. And the sooner the spins, the better.

STRUCTURE IN TELEVISION SCRIPTS

A DRAMA PILOT

The structure of a one-hour drama pilot is similar to a one-hour episode. The only difference is the one-hour pilot introduces the theme of the show, the characters, the tone, a sample episode, and the arc of the five seasons.

One of the most important questions to answer is if your pilot is self-contained or serial. Next, you must determine theme, characters, and tone.

THE THEME OF THE SHOW

The theme is basically the concept for a one-hour drama pilot—a procedural, a family drama, or a high concept.

In a procedural show (i.e., cop, FBI, U.S. Marshall, private detective, etc.), the narrative of the show is to solve a crime. Think *CSI* or its many knock-offs.

In a family drama, like *Big Love* or *Brothers and Sisters,* intertwining relationships and stories often combine drama, comedy, and heartstrings.

The show can be high concept. This is a term seldom used anymore, but means the show rides on the concept as being extraordinary. For example, *Lost* or *Medium.* These are shows that are highly unlikely, rarely even close to reality, but we love the idea so much the audience suspends disbelief and just goes with it.

THE CHARACTERS

Recurring characters must be introduced and we must want to follow them through the course of five seasons. We must not only care about the characters, but we must want to stay with them for a long time and see how they change.

How can we care about characters we've just met in one pilot episode? That is your job. If you create cardboard cutouts, chances are the pilot won't even get past the assistant's desk. If it does manage to get produced, it won't make it past season one.

THE TONE

The tone is a little understood part of the one-hour pilot. You need to know if you are writing for network or cable, because there is a world of difference, and it all comes down to tone. Many cable executives have little patience for network concepts, and the reverse is true also—network executives do not like to read or be pitched cable shows.

The difference is that networks try to stay in the boundaries of family viewing. When networks have shows that push the boundaries, they try to program the shows in late night times (after 9 p.m.).

Cable shows, on the other hand, follow very few guidelines or boundaries. Cable shows generally don't blink at profanity, blood, violence, and nudity. They have little patience for family-skewed audiences.

Is the tone of your pilot more baseball and cherry pie, or is it more cage fighting and stripper poles? Figure out your tone and you'll help your focus—and you'll know exactly where to make your pitch.

I have made the mistake of sending or pitching a family show to a cable executive, and was nearly thrown out on my ear. Trust me, this is a big deal.

SELF-CONTAINED

A self-contained, one-hour drama means there will be an "A" story that has a beginning, middle, and an end. The lawyer will try the case to win or lose. The cop will catch the criminal. The psychic will solve the murder. Next week, in the next episode, you'll have a new "A" story with its own beginning, middle, and end.

In the 1960s, '70s, '80s, and most of the '90s, the majority of one-hour dramas were self-contained. Shows such as *Mannix* or *The Man from U.N.C.L.E.* or *Barnaby Jones* all solved the case. These shows made great syndications because the audience could sit down and watch any episode and be satisfied with an ending. If they missed an episode or two, no big deal, they'd just catch it on a rerun and not lose a beat by the time they watched the show again.

SERIAL ONE-HOUR DRAMAS

Conversely, serial one-hour dramas have an overarching storyline that encompasses the whole season or series. If you miss an episode, you're lost. Shows like this leave the audience hanging after an episode, hungry for the next one to see what happens.

Shows like *Lost* or *24* or *The Sopranos* or *The Wire* gave the audience little satisfaction from watching a random episode. You sit down to watch the show, but there is no ending to the "A" story, at least not right away. Sure, there are "B" and "C" stories in each episode that have a beginning, middle, and end, but the big story unravels slowly, like *Lost.*

I tried for years to watch *Lost*. Every time I tried, I *was* lost. This makes the viewer (me) want to rush out to buy the entire season just to understand one episode.

WRITE A SAMPLE EPISODE

All development executives for network and cable shows ask the same question, "Where are we going every week?" This means they want to know what will happen, generally speaking, each week. A sample episode will give them a good idea of the answer to that question.

I have read very good pilots that fail to insert a sample episode. If your show is going to be a procedural, then you have to solve a crime in your pilot episode. If there is going to be a treasure hunt every week, take the reader or audience on a treasure hunt in your pilot. Show the decision-makers what will happen each week by providing a sample episode.

THE ARC OF THE SHOW

The last thing that must be clear in your pilot, (especially in the pitch) is what the arc of the entire show will be. That means you must know and present where the characters and theme of the show are going to start and end after 100 episodes. What happens in the beginning? What happens in the middle? How does it all end?

Your pilot episode might be the most dazzling piece of writing the execs have seen since the beginning of time, but if you have no story that will take an audience on a long ride (and therefore make an indecent amount of money for the execs), your writing won't matter squat. They're looking for the next long-running series (think *CSI* or *Law and Order* or *Cold Case*) and really, they're hoping you are presenting it to them on a silver platter. Don't let them down.

GENERAL STRUCTURE OF A ONE-HOUR PILOT

The general structure of a one-hour pilot is composed of a teaser and five or six acts, though by the time you read this book, this may have changed. Do the research; stay on top of television act breaks. Things will change radically when commercials are obsolete, because all advertising will be in product placement (i.e., a Coke bottle on the detective's desk).

TEASER: Page 1 to Page 7; End of Teaser (Act Out)

ACT ONE: Page 7 to Page 17; End of Act One (Act Out)

ACT TWO: Page 18 to Page 28; End of Act Two (Act Out)

ACT THREE: Page 29 to Page 39; End of Act Three (Act Out)

ACT FOUR: Page 40 to Page 48; End of Act Four (Act Out)

ACT FIVE: Page 49 to Page 56; End of Act Five (Act Out)

(ACT 6 is optional)

ACT SIX: Page 57 to Page 62; End of Act Six

Another way to structure a pilot is in six straight acts, with no teaser. Just jump right in:

SIX STRAIGHT ACTS

ACT ONE: Page 1 to Page 14; End of Act One (Act Out)

ACT TWO: Page 15 to Page 25; End of Act Two (Act Out)

ACT THREE: Page 26 to Page 36; End of Act Three (Act Out)

ACT FOUR: Page 37 to Page 45; End of Act Four (Act Out)

ACT FIVE: Page 46 to Page 53; End of Act Five (Act Out)

ACT SIX: Page 54 to Page 60; End of Act Six

ACT OUTS

The most important part of television writing is not the structure, but the act outs (commercial breaks). In the days when dinosaurs roamed the earth, the commercial breaks were meant to advertise and allow people to go to the refrigerator.

When there were only three prime time network channels, the commercials were meant to entertain and sell cigarettes. The half-hour break was the most important break. It was the opportunity to get someone to change the station and drive the Neilson ratings up after the half-hour break. Hence, cars exploded and people got shot on the 30-minute cue.

Today, there are so many channels and recordable options that commercials have lost their ability to hold people from channel surfing or skipping the ads all together. Most people even watch shows with the remotes in their hands. The act outs, not the commercials, are meant to hold people in their seats. The end of each act now has to be compelling enough to keep viewers from changing the channel.

Now showrunners—the person assigned to run the show—want all the writers to come up with the strongest act out of each commercial break. When writers sit in the writers' room and break the story, it is all centered around each act break.

THE "A" and "B" and "C" STORIES

On self-contained shows, the "A" story has a beginning, middle, and end. Therefore the cop will chase the murderer and catch the murderer within one episode. Dr. House must find the disease and find the cure in one hour.

The "B" and "C" stories can be pushed through the next episode, and the next, and all season if needed. In the writers' room, the writers break down the "A" stories along with the "B" and "C" stories. Once this is done, they must figure out which one has the best act out.

To understand this concept, let's use *The Weary Detective* as an example of a one-hour TV drama break down.

THE WEARY DETECTIVE

Referencing our detective story from the "Structure" chapter in this book, our detective has lost the feeling for being a cop. He wants to focus on repairing his relationships with his wife and daughter, but obstacles ensue—

particularly, a big murder case involving his brother-in-law as the main suspect.

In the end of the episode, our protagonist follows his instincts and finds the missing element that ties the brother-in-law's mistress to a string of murders—but the audience knows he must overcome big obstacles to repair his personal life. But at least the case is solved. Next week, there will be another.

HOW TO BREAK THIS DOWN IN THE TELEVISION WRITERS' ROOM

It's nine o'clock in the morning, so the writers finish their coffee and bagels, and then wander into the writers' room. Eight writers and a showrunner sit at conference tables formed in a circle, and talk about current TV shows and news for about 45 minutes. The subject finally turns to "Episode 103" (the third episode in the new season of the new TV show).

Robert and Linda were assigned "Episode 103." Robert was assigned the "A" story; Linda was assigned the "B" and "C" stories. Robert picks up his tools (erasable color markers) and goes to white board number one. Linda takes her tools (erasable color markers) to white board number two. They each begin listing the beats of the "A," "B," and "C" (and sometimes "D") stories. Beats are the bullet points of each scene.

Robert writes:

"A" STORY BEATS

1) Someone finds a dead body and reports it.

2) Our detective talks to his partner about retiring. The murder case comes across their desk.

3) Detective and his partner go see the crime scene.

4) Detective finds out FBI has been tracking case; may be serial killer.

5) A clue points to a suspect—the detective's brother-in-law.

6) Detective goes with the FBI to see brother-in-law. The brother-in-law's wife (detective's wife's sister) wants to know what this is all about.

7) Brother-in-law is interrogated by FBI as detective watches. Detective has to go with FBI to search his brother-in-law's home while sister-in-law watches.

8) Detective follows brother-in-law and discovers he's having an affair.

9) A clue comes across detective's desk that may be his alibi.

10) Detective interrupts rendezvous between brother-in-law and mistress. The mistress tells detective she was with brother-in-law night of last murder.

11) There is a lead that points to female suspect. DNA doesn't match brother-in-law.

12) Detective follows hunch; follows brother-in-law's mistress.

13) Detective ties clue to mistress. He arrests mistress.

Linda writes:

"B" STORY BEATS

1) Detective's wife tells him she wants to separate.

2) Detective and wife meet at restaurant where they were engaged.

3) Detective cooks nice dinner; tells wife and daughter that brother-in-law is suspect.

4) Detective comes home with flowers; finds empty house.

5) Detective tells wife he loves her. She says her love is gone.

6) Detective calls wife and asks if there is someone else.

7) Detective goes to wife's work; finds her cozy with associate.

8) Detective threatens associate in bar.

9)   Detective comes home; wife has moved in with her sister.

10)   Detective goes to brother-in-law's house to warn wife that there is an FBI investigation.

11)   Detective tells wife he has quit his job for her; he wants to start over.

"C" STORY BEATS

1)   Detective gets call from teacher, who tells him that his daughter is failing.

2)   Detective meets with teacher and finds daughter has not been attending school.

3)   Detective confronts daughter. They have a verbal battle.

4)   Detective receives phone call from hospital. Daughter has overdosed.

5)   Detective goes to hospital with wife.

6)   Daughter's boyfriend visits detective; tells him daughter is pregnant.

7)   Detective takes daughter to a counselor.

8)   Detective tells daughter for first time that he loves her.

Now that the beats for Episode 103 have been put up and agreed with in the writers' room, all the writers stare at the board and begin to think about the next (most important) step.

WHAT ARE THE ACT OUTS?

The following is a simplified version, without writers' room swearing, coffee cups thrown against the wall, and long, exhausting breaks to call individual therapists.

Let's do a teaser and five acts (or six acts).

TEASER

"A" Story

1) A dead body.

2) Detective tells partner he can't wait to retire. The detectives pull the murder case.

3) Detectives go to crime scene.

"B" Story

1) Detective receives a cell phone call while at crime scene. Wife wants to talk. Detective says, "I'm too

busy, gotta' dead body staring at me." Wife asks, "Are you too busy to get a divorce?"

END OF TEASER

ACT ONE

(Note: A famous television show creator taught me, "Always take an audience where they want to follow." We introduced that the detective's wife wants a divorce—so we can't stray too far from that.)

"B" Story

2)   Detective takes wife to their favorite restaurant. He tries to charm her but he's way late and out of practice. Things begin to thaw out between strained husband and wife, when detective receives a telephone call.

"A" Story

4)   Detective and partner get pulled into Watch Commander's office; FBI agents are there. The case the detective has pulled is a suspected serial killer. Detective is pissed. Office Sergeant tells detective he

has a phone call. Detective excuses himself to take it—and is surprised to hear high school principal inform him that detective's daughter is in a lot of trouble.

"C" Story

1) Detective tells principal he will be right there. He leaves everyone waiting to investigate and discuss the murder case. Watch Commander is mad as hell that detective left.

2) Principal tells detective that daughter has not been attending school. Detective then receives telephone call from his partner who tells him he's got good news and bad news. Partner tells detective he must come back to Division before they are both fired.

"A" Story

5) Detective comes back to Police Division to have private consultation with his partner, who tells the detective the good news is they have a prime suspect. Detective asks, "What is the bad news?" Partner shows detective a picture of suspect, and it is the detective's brother-in-law.

(Note: You are a writer in the writers' room and you have to participate. Do you suggest this is a strong Act Out? If you want to keep your job, yes!)

END OF ACT ONE (Strong Act Out—Hooray!)

This is how we break down story in the writers' room, and this is how we approach writing episodes and one-hour drama pilots.

Exercise: Finish beating out the rest of the story and find the best Act Outs for this episode. You are now in the writers' room and developing a pilot or episode for a one-hour drama.

Oh yes, my friend, it is indeed an outline, isn't it? This is what is done in the professional writers' world/room before you get to sit in your chair and actually start the magic of writing. It's called preparation, and it's where the magic begins.

OUTLINES

People frequently ask me whether or not they should write an outline for a feature film or a television pilot. This question makes the hairs on the back of my neck stand up. I hate outlines (also known as "beat sheets") with a passion.

When a studio, network, or producer asks me to do an outline, my stomach twists into knots. There have been several times that a mandatory outline has been written into my contract for a writing assignment. My teeth automatically begin to grind. So I'm going to shout from the mountaintop my disdain for writing outlines. And when someone asks me if they should do it, I grit my teeth and say, "Absolutely."

One time I was hired to write the remake of a 1970's feature film, and the producer insisted I do an outline, so it was written into my contract. This is not unusual, and happens 90 percent of the time. The only problem was, there were five producers on the project, and my outline had to be approved before they all signed off on it. Only then would I be commenced (given permission to start) to write the screenplay.

Yes, you guessed it—five producers meant five different outlines, which, by the way, is against WGA (Writers Guild of America) rules. Hint: if you want to keep your job on a writing assignment, you often have to break the rules. Honor your union, the WGA, but don't be a tattletale. Make your agents fight against any abuse, but do your best to stay on the project (i.e., write a few more outlines and drafts, or it will become another writer's project).

When I finally delivered the outline that four of the producers approved, those four producers took the outline to the fifth producer (the one signing everyone's checks). The fifth producer hated the outline and I had to start over. All told, I wrote eight outlines before all the producers signed off to let me begin writing the screenplay.

Is this against the rules? Yes. Does it happen all the time? Yes. Is there something you can do about it? Yes. You can report the production company to the union and kiss your writing career goodbye.

This is why I loathe writing outlines. So why do I recommend writing them? Because as tedious as they are, and a time-drain, when you have completed the outline, you can fly through the script. Why? Because you know where you are going. You know the beginning, middle, and end of your story. It takes the pressure off your shoulders and you can just write. Most of the time you will make changes, but it's because you are on course.

Confession: Every time I didn't know my beginning, middle, and end, I never completed the screenplay. Every time I knew the beginning and middle, I never completed the screenplay. And every time I knew the end of my story, I completed the damn screenplay. Yes, 80 percent of the time you know your ending, you can finish the story. If you don't know where you are going, it will be right off the end of a cliff.

Do I hate writing outlines? Yes, with a passion. Do I recommend writing outlines? Yes, with double passion. Do I recommend writing countless outlines when you get hired to write a movie? Only if you want to get paid and keep working.

The time frame for an outline to be finished and submitted for approval is usually one week. When you receive notes, you have to make the changes within a couple days at the most. Once your outline is approved and signed off, you usually get six to ten weeks to turn in a first draft of a screenplay. This is why I tell my students to practice writing a feature screenplay in no more than three months. When you get your first job, this is the average amount of time you get to turn in a first draft.

Television writing is a little different. When you are a writer on a TV show, you must turn in an outline to the studio and network. The showrunner will often call the network and studio to pitch your outline. If there are notes, it is good to get them before you start writing. Also, the timing of start to finish goes so fast that if you cannot keep up, you will be fired.

On most television shows, you have one week to get your script idea to the line producer, get the outline completed and approved, and finish the script. Once the executive producer and showrunner approve your idea, you have to turn in your outline in less than 24 hours.

You receive notes and have to come back with a revised outline in only a few hours. Once the outline is approved, you have to write a 60-page script in three to four days. You turn in your script for notes and approval, and once you receive them, you have to make the changes in less than a day. If you can't keep up with this pace, you will be replaced. This is why I tell my students to practice writing a pilot in one week or less.

When you are hired to write on a show, you will be expected to meet your deadline once your episode comes into the rotation. No excuses. Let's say there are 22 or 26 shows to write in a season. With eight writers, you will average two to three episodes per season. When it's your episode, write super fast and super well.

WHAT IS A SCRIPT OUTLINE?

An outline can be written in several forms. The most important part of an outline is to let the producers and directors know what direction you're heading.

BULLET POINTS

I personally like to give a simple listing of bullet point scenes. This does not mean you should write a list of ALL the scenes—it means you are listing the important scenes in each act. If you are writing a feature film, just list the bullet point scenes of Act One and Act Two and Act Three. Act Two will have more scenes than Act One and Act Three, because Act Two is the longest act in a three-act feature film format.

FOR EXAMPLE:

Let's say we're making a feature film out of the detective story I made up in the "Film and Television Structure" chapters. If I was putting together a feature film outline based on *The Weary Detective,* it would be as follows:

ACT ONE

- Scene 1

A young woman goes running on a hiking trail. She stumbles over a branch and falls face first. She brushes herself off, goes back to find her shoe by the branch, and sees it is not a branch she stumbled on, but the leg of a dead body.

- Scene 2

A detective (our hero) puts his feet up on his desk and stares at the wall clock. His partner tells him to stop staring at the clock. The phone rings, and the two detectives look at the telephone. The detectives both roll their eyes and pray it's nothing important. The detective (our hero) answers the telephone with his fingers crossed. He's unhappy upon hearing a murder reported.

- Scene 3

At the crime scene (where the body was discovered), the detective and his partner stare at the dead body. The detective's cell phone rings. He answers to discover his wife wants a divorce.

This is a simple example of an outline, or a beat sheet.

A TELEVISION OUTLINE

A television outline is a little different (see the chapter on "Television Structure").

In a one-hour drama that has a teaser plus five or six acts, you can write the outline the same way. Or you can write an even looser outline, such as we did on *The Unit*.

EXAMPLE for *The Unit* outline:

TEASER

- A female jogger trips over a dead body on a hiking trail.

- The detective and his partner receive a phone call. They pull the murder case.

- At the crime scene, the detective receives a cell phone call from his wife. She asks him for a divorce.

END OF TEASER

Different television shows have different rules for outlines. The same is true for feature films. The main key to writing good outlines is to only write the bullet points. Do not go into intricate detail. The more you write in an outline, the more subjected you are to criticism. To keep the criticism of your outline at a manageable level, keep your writing short and concise.

TV AND MOVIE BIBLES

I have been told a television "bible" is a document that contains the idea for a television show, the cast of characters, and a breakdown of possible episodes. Apparently, some of these bibles even go into great detail about the background of each character, and include possible episodes for as many as two to five seasons. Sometimes they are created for movies.

This is hearsay because I have not actually seen these lengthy, detailed bibles. I've only heard about them from new writers who ask me about them, and from film festivals that dedicate entire panels on them.

The truth is that in all the years I've been writing screenplays on assignments for television and movies, including the pilots I've sold, I have never written a bible. In fact, no producer, network, studio, or literary agent has ever requested I write a bible. None. Ever.

In actuality, I don't know how to write something I have never been required to do. Had I been required to write a television or movie bible, I would have taken the time to learn how to write one. I would also teach my students how to compose one. But believe me, if they were paramount in selling scripts or being hired to write scripts, I'm sure someone would have advised me to learn how to write one.

The last television show I sold was to 20ᵗʰ Century Fox. I went in and pitched my idea to the producer. He said I should go home and prepare to write the pilot while they (the producer and studio) negotiated with my agent. Once a deal was in place, I was required to write the pilot. The word "bible" never came up.

It is certainly true television bibles can give the writer some background on his or her characters. It also can be useful in developing a voice for your characters and over-arching stories throughout the seasons. I'm sure it is very helpful to writers to know all these things in order to feel they know their stories and characters.

This has never been critical for me. What is critical when I sit down to write a movie, television episode, or pilot is that there is a reason I am writing a character into a scene.

I only write characters into scenes when they have pressing and immediate needs to be in the scene.

This means my only concern is what the characters want now and why I am writing about them now—not their histories or their mothers' histories. My characters must do something to achieve their immediate, pressing needs. If there is no immediate and pressing need, there is no need for the character to be in the scene. This means they must act immediately. There is no other reason to put them into a scene.

For example, Stephanie has 30 seconds to put out a fire in the kitchen or she and her children will burn to a crisp. The fact that Stephanie was a graduate of an Ivy League school and her sister died of a tragic rafting trip 17 years ago has nothing to do with why I am writing about Stephanie now. The only reason the audience should care about Stephanie is to know if she can put out the fire in the kitchen and save herself and her children. That is drama. Though tragic that Stephanie had a sister who died 17 years ago, it does not solve the immediate and urgent reasons Stephanie must be written into a scene.

If by any chance I decide to write a scene outside Stephanie's home where two firemen are having a conversation about why Stephanie may not be able to save her kids because her sister died tragically 17 years ago, this is called exposition and should be left out of all screenplays from now until eternity. Exposition is information. Information is not drama.

I have written a one- to three-page outline or synopsis about my movie or television show. I don't call it a bible. I called it an outline or a synopsis. In the outline or synopsis I write about the story, especially the small story. I write about the characters, including what they want, why they can't get it, and why the audience should care. I write about where the characters begin and where they end.

I study what I have written and then pitch to a hopefully captivated audience at a production office, network, or studio. I never, ever, leave my one to three pages behind. If they did not understand something or need further clarification, I want them to ask me (which means someone is interested) or I want them to call me back or ask my agent (which also means someone is interested).

To be clear, I recommend you do *not* leave anything behind after you make a pitch. When you leave something behind (such as an outline or synopsis), you leave it open to be slaughtered, mangled, and criticized. The more you write down and show to a production company, network, or studio, the more vulnerable you and your work are.

You are welcome to create a bible, but don't expect to be asked for one or for it to be an integral part of the industry. And if you do write one, don't leave it behind at a pitch.

HOW TO PITCH

THE ODDS OF THE PITCH

In the entertainment industry, pitching is presenting your idea to a producer or studio with the goal of selling your idea, concept, and/or script. I'll define this more later, but first you should know that pitching will be as important to you as writing. Your agent will get you in some doors, but you will be responsible for making "the sale." To increase your odds, you'd better know how to pitch.

If an NBA player makes 45 percent of his three-point shots, he's considered one of the best of all time. If a Major League Baseball player gets a hit 30 percent of the time, he may be inducted into the Hall of Fame. If a writer, producer, or director sells 10 percent of his or her pitches, he or she is living on top of the hill in the biggest house.

I have conservatively sold one pitch a year for 15 years. In a good year, with a stellar agent, I've pitched as many as 30 times. Pitching is to a writer like auditioning is to an actor. With both careers, the odds are stacked against you, but when you win, you win big. That's why it's so important to know what you're doing when you pitch—to increase your odds and ultimately make a sale.

PITCHING FOR ASSIGNMENT WRITING

Many people outside the film and television business do not understand what defines a pitch. More than that, most do not understand how a professional screenwriter makes the greatest percent of his or her income.

A screenwriter does not make money selling his or her ideas. Unlike what was portrayed in the movie *The Player*, writers do not generate the most amount of consistent income by pitching lofty ideas such as, "Well, Sam, it's a cross between *Pretty Woman* and *Predator.*"

Writers make the greatest percent of their income by being hired on assignment. An assignment is an open writing position that has been "green lit" to hire a writer for services on contract. Most contracts are categorized as a "three-step deal."

Once the production company, studio, or network has approved the writer, the writer's representation (agent, manager, or entertainment attorney) clearly defines the terms and gets the best deal for the writer. This process sometimes goes smoothly, and the contracts are signed in a matter of weeks. Other times, it takes light years for everyone to agree and sign off on contracts.

One time, a showrunner for a new television drama called my agent to offer me a job as a writer on the show. He told my agent in good faith (even though contracts had not been agreed to or signed) that I should go ahead and join the staff before my deal closed. On good faith, I got into my car and started to drive to the production office to meet the staff and read the episodes that had already been drafted. Halfway there, my agent called and said to turn my car around. The showrunner was not able to close a deal with one of the key directors who was at the same agency as me. The showrunner announced a moratorium on any writers, actors, and directors from my agency.

By the time I returned home and pulled into my driveway, my agent called again to tell me to turn back around and go to my new place of employment. The showrunner and the director settled on their contract, and the moratorium was lifted. Yes, in Hollywood, anything can happen, and it does.

Now the ink has dried, and the writer is gainfully employed writing a movie, or writing for a new television series. What happened in between, and how does pitching come into play?

A green lit writing assignment means the money is in place to hire a writer. This includes an idea, a television show, a book adaptation to film, or a biography (or true story or historical event). All green lit writing assignments start with a pitch. The pitch is made by the writer in the interview by potential employers. This is the process for a film assignment, in a nutshell:

1. The potential employer (i.e., the studio, network, or production company) will get financing to hire a writer for a project.

2. The potential employer will then "read" an average of 20 or 30 potential writers. These writers are selected

based on a number of unique reasons. It could be credits (based on box office hits and nominations for awards), reputation (great to work with), or proven ability in the show's genre and/or price (the more hits and nominations, the higher the price for the writer).

3. The potential employer will narrow down the field to a small selection of his favorite writers.

4. The potential employer will then call these few writers in for an interview (writing samples are not enough).

5. The writer(s) will come in for an interview and "pitch." The potential employer will interview the narrowed list of writers and ask each writer a few questions about the project. Writers with good agents or managers will be well prepared to speak intelligently on the subject of the project in the interview. Yes, panic ensues as the writer then has to learn as much about the subject as she or he can in a short amount of time in order to give a "take" on the subject. A "take" is the writer's pitch on how he or she would go about writing the cinematic story of the open assignment. This is a definite pitch, so don't attempt to "wing it." Be prepared.

6. The potential employer will select a writer and offer an assignment deal.

The same process occurs in the television world. It's a little different but it goes as follows:

1. A new show will be announced during May "pick-ups." This is when all the new and old shows are announced. Cancellations mean more new shows.

2. A new show has to be staffed with writers. The selection process begins.

3. Several dozen writers are read, and several dozen writers are interviewed. If you make the interview, realize that your writing is good enough to be considered for a position.

4. When the selection field is narrowed, the show will send you (the writer) the pilot to watch and read.

5. After you've done this, they will call you into the office and ask for your "take" or "pitch" on how you would contribute to the show.

Pitching is one of the most pervasive aspects of the film and television world. If you are the best writer on the planet, great—but if you can't present this award-worthy writing or your ideas in person, you might as well become an accountant. Directors, camera crew, and editors all have to "pitch" or "sell" themselves and their work to get the jobs.

MY PITCH EQUALS MY JOBS

The bottom line is that I learned early on that writing skill is only half the battle to make it in this business. I had to perfect my pitch—and that has made all the difference. You would not believe how many good writers are very bad at pitching, and yes, it costs them jobs.

Because I pitch *and* write well, I have been hired to write book adaptations such as *Dangerous Evidence* and *The Last Shot.* I have been hired to write biographies such as *The Louis Armstrong Story* and *Three Friends* (based on the lives of Coretta Scott King, Myrlie Evers, and Betty Shabazz).

I have been hired to write fictional concepts such as *Too Young to Marry* and *Heist.* And very rarely, I've been hired to write my own ideas such as *The Simple Life of Noah Dearborn* and *Gus.* I have been hired to write for television shows such as *The Unit* and *Medium.* And, I've been hired to write film scripts currently in pre-production.

I got all these jobs by pitching.

Like writing, pitching is a craft. It is a skill. It is a learned skill that comes from several trial and error moments—knees shaking, in front of people or the person holding the keys to the automobile (your paycheck and career).

SOMETIMES YOU GET LUCKY

Not a lot of people fall off the truck, dust themselves off, push the saloon doors open, and sell a terrific pitch—but sometimes you get lucky. It happens.

GENERALS ALWAYS TURN INTO A PITCH SESSION

My first pitch was in front of a studio executive at Columbia Pictures. My agent had only told me I was going to a "general" with an executive at Columbia Pictures. A general is supposed to be a meet and greet with someone in the business—usually with a junior executive, sometimes with a mover and shaker (remember, the junior executives are the future movers and shakers).

In this particular general meeting, I had no idea what I was doing or going to say. It did not help in the least bit that I saw Barbra Streisand in the lobby just five minutes before my appointment. My teeth rattled and my knees squeaked when the studio executive's assistant came to show me into the office. The assistant asked me if I wanted some coffee, water, tea, or juice. I screamed, "Yes!" at the nervous top of my lungs.

When I sat down in front of the perfectly tailored man with his fingers steepled in front of his nose, I was nervous— and distracted. Babs was super fine; I wanted to scream, "Damn, Babs is fine for her age!" Fortunately, I refrained.

When the executive asked me if I wanted to pitch something to him, I was naïve enough to say, "Yeah, sure." My brain racked and nearly exploded when I barked some nonsensical diatribe in streams of nervous spit.

I walked out of the Thalberg building on the Sony Studio lot with a $40,000 deal to go write what I just pitched.

Honestly, I barely remembered what I said. It went something like this: "I would love to write a story about a stranger who wanders into a small, one stop-sign town and seems to solve everyone's problems. When the stranger has just made everyone's lives seem to become magical, they discover the stranger is a wanted man, one on the run."

That's it. That was my very first pitch. Lord knows why I was offered money to go write it. I did. The script was called *Gus,* and the movie was never made.

I have no idea how the stars aligned that day. I have no idea why I stumbled into the saloon and the barkeep said the drinks were on the house. What I do know is between then and now, I honed my skills. I made an ass of myself, failed miserably pitching in rooms, and somehow, around one in 30 times, I sold more than a dozen more pitches in my career.

ALWAYS BE PREPARED TO PITCH

I also know I have to always be prepared to pitch, even if the meeting is not supposed to be a pitch. More often than not, a general meeting will slowly (like quicksand) turn into a pitch meeting. Here are two examples:

One time I had not seen a friend in several years. She had rocketed up the ladder in the Hollywood fast lane. The first time I met her was in a general meeting. She was a development executive for a film company. We talked for hours, and later became social friends. Neither one of us had worked in television when we met. We lost track of one another, as friends do.

One California T-shirt day in the middle of winter, we ran into one another at a coffee shop. When I asked her what she was doing now, she told me she was president of the television division at a major production company. I said that was a coincidence, because I had spent the last six years in television. She said, "Perfect. Tell your agent to set up a meeting with me."

I didn't think much of it. A meeting was scheduled, and I really believed I was going to just shoot the breeze in her office like old times. When I arrived at her company, I was quickly escorted into a conference room.

The hairs stood up on the back of my neck when I saw that half dozen empty seats had a pen and note pad in front of them. Next came the procession of people in front of my old friend. She sat down, crossed her legs, and asked, "So, what are you pitching today?"

I stammered, stumbled, and fumbled my way through a very awkward meeting.

REFRAIN FROM THROTTLING YOUR AGENT

Another time, my agent regaled me about how much a production company, fresh off an Academy Award for best picture, loved me more than sliced bread. That's a lot, right? He waxed me with how much they enjoyed my writing samples and how much they looked forward to getting in business with me on a project. Then he said the magical words, "Dude, these guys really want to pitch something to you."

I asked, "What?"

My agent said he didn't know, but a meeting was set by the end of the week.

Of course I sauntered into this production company feeling like a Playboy centerfold at a frat party. I think when the receptionist asked me if she could help me, I really believe I winked at her and replied, "Oh, yes you can."

My head bounced off both walls as I was led into the conference room. This time there were no note pads and pens at the ready. Good start, right? The owners came into the room with two assistants; smiles were wide as the Mississippi River.

We did the perfect preamble (which, as I've always taught my students, is the most important part of any good pitch meeting). We glided through the introductions and preamble, and then the room went silent and everyone was staring at me. It was like the old western movies where guns were drawn around the campfire, and there is always the stupid one who brought a knife to the gun fight. That was me, only I wasn't holding anything remotely sharp.

There I was, looking at everyone looking at me. Then one of the owners gave me an encouraging smile and said, "So, your agent said you have a wonderful pitch for us today."

My mouth dropped. I thought of manslaughter, but my agent was miles away. I'm guessing the parable of this story is to always keep a pitch in your back pocket.

PREAMBLE IS IMPORTANT

One of the most important aspects of pitching is the preamble. It will make or break your pitch meeting.

When you walk into a room, you have already been invited. Somehow, someway, someone got you into the room. When you walk into that room, you are immediately judged. They are looking at what you are wearing, how you groom and carry yourself, your intelligence, and your sense of humor. Why? Because they want to know immediately, do they like you? They want to know if they want to spend six months to a year or longer with you. So the first thing that comes out of your mouth is the most important.

No one should walk into the room and launch into the story. Your preamble must massage your entrance into the room. As you look around the room, smile and say something warm and interesting to everyone present.

I have walked into the room and said, "Oh my gawd, I am so sleep deprived. My new baby refuses to sleep." Yes, that was it. That was my preamble and the room lit up with empathy. The men and women sat back, relaxed, and then launched into stories about their own children. If they didn't have children, their sisters or brothers or bosses had children. The ice was broken; they liked me before I sat down.

I have also walked into a room and said, "That was the worst traffic I have seen in my life." Everyone in the room slapped their notepads and launched into their own traffic stories. Again, everyone was talking as I took my seat.

I have walked into a room, noticed that the two guys waiting were both athletically built, and said, "I will never play golf again." The men were both golfers, and yes, I got the job.

Okay, so you've been brilliant in your preamble and there is an awkward silence. You know the time has come to put up or shut up. Before you start your pitch, make sure you assess the room, and make sure to pitch to everyone.

Sometimes nerves take over and you focus on only one person in the room. Big mistake. Pitch to everyone there, not just the pretty girl or the person with the most expensive suit or watch. Don't ignore the assistant with the notepad. Pitch to the boss, the assistant, the assistant boss, whoever is there. They will all appreciate your professionalism.

Seriously, this is important. I have been nervous and focused in on just one person, and it was the wrong person. I did not get the job.

Next, check your mental clock. Make sure you know what 20 minutes means—it's the magic number. Not 20 minutes from when you sit down, but 20 minutes from when you enter the room. The people you're pitching to have already heard 50 pitches that week. If your pitch is great, they'll want more. If it stinks, they'll be glad you kept it short.

Now you're back into that uncomfortable silence and someone will fold their hands and ask, "So, we hear you have something to pitch us today." This is when you remember what you read in *Beyond Screenwriting* in the beginning of the "Television Structure" chapter. By this time you have prepared and know your theme (concept), characters, and tone.

If you are good, you will launch into your pitch with ease, poise, and clarity. If you are great (a black belt) you will launch into a quick, no more than two-minute mini-story on how you came to the idea or pitch. Sometimes your reason for telling the story will be more captivating than the story itself. Even if your pitch stinks, you may be invited back because you are so professional and so charming. Seriously.

HIGH CONCEPT DRIVEN

If your pitch is high concept, be prepared to pack your punch by selling the uniqueness of it. In fact, make sure your idea is so unique that you'll blow them away just telling it.

For example, a writer pitched the concept that a man has the ability to bring dead people back to life for a few minutes by touching them. This high concept (way out there) idea became a television show called *Pushing Daisies*.

If the network or studio doesn't buy the idea, there is no need to talk about the characters.

CHARACTER DRIVEN

If your pitch is a family drama, biopic, or someone searching for a hidden treasure, it is driven by the richness of the characters. Make sure the characters are vivid, interesting, and flawed. Now, present your pitch.

Start with the concept, and then talk about one or two characters the listeners will care about. Next, briefly tell the beginning, middle, and end of your story. Make sure you hit the small story (see the "Story" chapter). Tell it like you are telling a story to your best friend. Be eloquent, relaxed, and enthusiastic—and act as if you've done it a thousand times.

Once you are finished, make sure you politely stand and leave before you are asked to leave. Never let the moment come where someone looks at his watch and calls an end to the meeting. Beat them to the punch.

If your exit is uncomfortable, then so will be the after-effect of your performance. Grab those nerves and get your behind out of that room, swiftly, and with poise. Like the late John Wooden said, "Be quick, but don't hurry." Be quick to shake hands and leave before you are asked to leave. When you do leave, don't hurry.

Go home and have a milkshake. You will hear in short order how the pitch went. Executives tend to pass quickly (say "no" to a pitch), so if you don't hear anything for a while, your pitch may be working its way up the ladder.

BEYOND SCREENWRITING

There are many little things in the way that you format your script that tell the network, producer, agent, studio, or literary manager whether you are a beginning or experienced writer.

Here are a few tips to get you started in the right direction.

SCENE HEADING

Only use one dash between location and time of day. No one uses two dashes, and I still don't know why it is an option in writing programs. Old school.

TIME OF DAY

Time of day should track throughout your story. If you write "Day," do not continue to write "Day" unless it's an entirely different day. There is no need to write "Morning" or "Afternoon" or "Evening." All the director wants to know is what lighting to set for the scene. There are two choices: "Don't need light setup—Day" or "need light set up—Night." The director only wants to know if it is light or dark.

CONTINUED, LATER, AND MOMENTS LATER

Never use these. Work harder. Let's say we end a scene with, "Payne snuffs his one cigarette in the ashtray, pulls the rifle in position, and looks to see if there is a shot." If we go out of the scene and come back to it to show passage of time, do not write "Later" in the scene heading. Instead, use action to explain. "Payne digs around in the over-filled (tar stained) ashtray for a long butt to smoke." Now the reader knows it is later because many cigarettes have been smoked.

ACTION

Only write action in action. Never write emotion in action. There is no use in writing, "Houston is terribly distraught, and his mind is still on his argument with Nell." This is not action; this is exposition that should be used only as a sleep aid.

DESCRIPTION

Too many beginning scriptwriters describe a character down to length and color of his or her nose hair. For example, Joey, 22 years old, red hair, thick eyebrows, pouty lips, one eyebrow always slightly raised, a city hitch in his step, and has three freckles under his left eye—walks into the room.

These details give away that the writer has not participated in many auditions or casting sessions. The fact is, the best actor who auditioned for the part usually gets the role. Joey's character may end up short and pudgy because the pudgy actor's audition blew away the casting director, producer, writer, and director. I have seen so many times where the description of the character ends up being nothing like the (beginning) writer described.

I have seen the character description call for a Chinese man, and the director decides at the last minute the character should be an African-American female. I have seen a tall, dark, and handsome role go to a short, blond, average actor whose charisma was off the charts.

Let's revisit the description of the Joey character. A seasoned writer would describe him this way: Joey, early-20's, walks into the room—looks around.

Only be specific if the character's scar or tattoo will help carry off the crime. In the television series *Prison Break*, for example, one of the characters had the tattoo of the prison floor plan on his back. This specific description drove all the episodes.

CHARACTER NAMES

Try to use variations in the first and last initials of characters. For example: Mark, Monroe, Michael, and Milford in one script will confuse the reader. When readers get confused, they stop reading. Jack, Arnold, Fred, Dolly, and Marcus all have different initials and do not sound the same.

Sometimes it's not just the first initials being the same that confuses readers. Names that sound too much the same, such as Harold and Arnold, can also confuse the reader and send him or her back to the beginning of the script. Using similar sounding names can break up the flow of the read, and believe me, most readers won't be patient enough to stick with your script if that happens. So yes, this is one time the writer should be anal. Stay away from Winston and Clinton. And Joan and Jane. I wouldn't even use Carol and Karen in the same script. Nor would I use Johnson and Washington.

Stay consistent with the names of characters. If your character's name is Detective John (Skip) Anderson, do not call him Skip and Detective Anderson and John. (Yes, I have seen this more times than I'd like to remember.)

Unusual names do get the gold star. Memorable is good. Atlas is better than Bob, and Sippy is better than Ned. My favorite name I'll always remember in a script is Rhee Joyce. It is perfectly professional to get creative with names.

PARENTHETICAL

Don't write paragraphs in a parenthetical. Joe (coughs, scratches, grabs his crotch, and looks at Sarah) is not okay. Keep words in a parenthetical brief, such as Joe (coughs) goes to the window. You can use emotion in parenthetical but do it (sparingly).

EXCLAMATIONS

Avoid the use of exclamations in a script. Trust the actor or actress to know how to use emphasis in dialogue.

Some writers go wild with exclamations and it looks like characters are screaming all the time.

"George!" "What!" "Get down!" "Never!"

It gives me and other readers a headache, and brands you as a beginner. Avoid it, or at least use sparingly.

PHONETICAL DIALOGUE

Do not write phonetically in dialogue. "Dog gummit, Bill, I feel like keeling you." Or even worse, "Meester Andrew, can chu give me a leetle more money?" These phonetics take away the emotion of the scene. It's all right to use descriptors (i.e., Spanish accent or Southern slang), but let novel writers wrestle with phonetic dialogue. You, as a screenwriter, can leave it to the actors to master.

KEEP DIALOGUE SPARSE

Finally, never dialogue your way through a story (unless your first name is Quentin and your last name is Tarantino, and you are so good at it that all is forgiven). All characters should speak only when they absolutely have to speak. Remember, when it comes to a screenplay, actions speak louder than words.

TRANSITION

I once had a director, Charles Dutton, call me to say, "Sterling, please get rid of all the Cut To's." This should tell you most of what you need to know about transitions. Use them sparingly or not at all. "Cut To" or "Dissolve To" or "Smash Cut To" all over a script is annoying and takes up page count space; however, sometimes they do have their place and are useful.

As a general rule I will use "Cut To" or "Dissolve To" if the story changes dramatically in time, space, and emotion. For example, I may use them if there is a significant passage of time such as weeks, months, or years.

Regarding space, if the scene goes from San Francisco to New York, I may tend to use "Cut To" or "Dissolve To." If the emotion of the story shifts greatly, like a key character dies or someone is taken without a trace, or after a rape or murder scene, then there needs to be a breather such as "Dissolve To."

Other than those special circumstances, always try to write an entire script without transitions. And when it becomes awkward and painful to not use a transition, then you have a green light to use one.

FLATLINE DIALOGUE (DON'T DO IT)

When all characters are smart or funny, or have witty dialogue, it flatlines a script. Your characters must sound like different people. They can't all have one "voice." Change it up. Have some smart, some dumb, some slow speaking, and some rattling on too fast.

LOG LINES

Very often when your screenplay goes up the chain of command, you or your agent will be called and asked, "What is the log line?" This means, what is an intriguing way to describe your screenplay in ONE LINE.

Log line does not mean, "My story is about a vet who never received love from his father, so he went on a rafting trip down the Nile and discovered he was in love with an alligator."

No. A log line should intrigue. For example, when the production company called to ask what was the log line of my high school undercover pilot (called *The 319*), my answer was: "In order to fool them, you have to become them."

Once, a studio called to ask what the log line was of my pilot I had just sold them (called *The Messenger*), about a man just getting out of prison with a list of favors for death row inmates. All the favors are a map to find the daughter who was kidnapped from him before he went to prison. My answer was: "They believe he had a book of favors; he knew he had a map."

SCRIPT REVISION COLOR CODES

When a screenwriter is commenced to write a film or an episode of a television show, each re-write is coded by color. Each color represents a stage in the draft process to reduce confusion, ensure everyone is referencing the same draft, and eventually get you to a final script. Get to know what the color sequence means so you can act professional and act like you've been there, done that.

first draft is white
first draft 1st revision is blue

first draft 2nd revision is pink
first draft 3rd revision is yellow
first draft 4th revision is green
first draft 5th revision is gold
first draft 6th revision is buff
first draft 7th revision is salmon
first draft 8th revision is cherry
first draft 9th revision is tan
second draft 1st revision is white
second draft 2nd revision is blue
second draft 3rd revision is pink
second draft 4th revision is yellow
second draft 5th revision is green
second draft 6th revision is gold
second draft 7th revision is buff
second draft 8th revision is salmon
second draft 9th revision is cherry
second draft 10th revision is tan
third draft 1st revision is white
third draft 2nd revision is blue
and so forth ...

When you get this far into rewrites, start looking for another writing gig.

One of my proudest moments as a writer was when I was writing on a television show, and my script went from First Draft 1st Revision to shooting the script.

BOTTLE AND SUBMARINE EPISODES

During the course of a 22-episode season, the line producer will storm into the writers' room or the show creator's office and yell, "We're over budget! We need a submarine episode!" This is a common occurrence because some episodes go over budget.

For example, when a popular and successful show is on the air, the budget may be $2 million an episode. This means the line producer has only $44 million to shoot the entire season. This is high, and reserved for very successful shows (and when shows become so successful that actors start asking for $1 million an episode, this is another problem altogether).

For a 22-episode season, the estimated cost per episode may be $2 million per episode. Episode 1 may cost $2.3 million. Episode 2 may cost $1.8 million. Episode 3 may cost $2.6 million. Episode 4 may cost $1.9 million. Is the show over budget? Yes, the show is over budget by $600,000.

Now the line producer looks at the budget for "Episode 5" and realizes he has only $1.4 million. So what does he do? He comes into the writers' room and says, "Bottle episode."

This means the writers have to write an episode that has no special effects, no super stunts, and no locations.

So how does this affect the writer? If the writer is worth his or her weight, he or she will come up with a "submarine" or "bottle" episode, where the entire episode is filmed simply within one location. So when you see your favorite show end up in a hostage situation on one location, or trapped in a building because a bomb is set to go off, or everyone is trapped in a bottle or a submarine, then you know a writer secured his or her job for the entire next season.

LOVE YOUR LINE PRODUCER

Many people believe the showrunner actually runs the show. This is a misnomer. The showrunner is the liaison between the network, studio, and creator of the show. He or she runs the writers' room, and is responsible for putting out the best episodes possible.

The person who really runs the show is the line producer. He or she has all the money. This means that he or she manages the cost and budget for writers, grips, prop masters, actors, sets, locations, and the whole nine yards.

I have seen the creator of a show ask the line producer if he could have a car chase, or have a character parachute off the building within an episode, or blow up a helicopter. And the line producer slowly shook his head and said, "No dice."

When I wrote for *The Unit,* I wrote a pivotal scene in one of my episodes where the bad guys are getting away with cases of surface-to-air missiles, the most feared weapon of homeland security. Someone with a working surface-to-air missile has the potential to bring down a commercial jet.

I wrote, "The team leader watched the helicopter pull way, then realized he'd only recovered one surface-to-air missile." So what does the team leader do? Yes, he must use the one remaining surface-to-air missile to shoot the helicopter down.

The line producer gently knocked on my door and said, "Sterling, we can't blow up a helicopter. That will cost more than the entire episode."

I was in a panic. This was the key moment at the end of my script. So I asked the line producer, "What if everyone turns their heads and we see the explosion off the reflection of the jeep?"

The line producer smiled and said, "Congratulations, Sterling. You just saved your episode."

Blowing up a helicopter costs a fortune, but seeing an explosion in a reflection only costs a few thousand dollars for the special effects department. Again, be nice to your line producer—he or she *really* runs the show.

POETRY AND NOVEL WRITING

When I first started writing screenplays, I was told over and over again that I wrote screenplays like a novel. I would smile, and my head would grow. Little did I realize, this was not a compliment. Translation: Your scripts are heady and drone on with too much detail.

Some writers are brilliant and write poetic or novelized stories. In this case, my best advice is to write poetry or a novel. Scripts must be as short and concise as possible. Yes, it still applies: Start a scene at the last minute, and get out of it as quickly as possible.

SOUND ADVICE

WHAT TO WRITE

In order to get an agent, you must have a solid writing sample. In order for your agent to get you work, you must have an inventory of writing samples. If you only have one script to peddle in this town, your chances of success are very limited.

WRITE WHAT YOU KNOW

That one solid writing sample, though, is vital. It has to be great. If you don't even have one script written yet, start now. Learn the mechanics of how to write screenplays, and then write what you know. This will be your calling card—your writing sample—and will represent you and your talent to everyone on the other side of that Hollywood wall.

WRITE WHAT YOU DON'T KNOW

Once you have written what you know, then you will have a writing sample. This will be the first of your writing sample inventory. Next, immediately write something you do not know. The reason you must immediately write what you do not know is because all professional screenwriters make the greatest percentage of their income by being hired to write something for someone else.

Writing about something you don't know is as easy as good research. Research is a crucial element of good screenwriting, and your ability to do it well (or not) will show up in your scripts. If you know about rodeos, and all five sample scripts are about rodeos, producers will view you as a very limited writer. If you write five scripts about five totally different subject matters, your versatility will be evident.

Over the years you must build an inventory. Every year my agent asks me, "Do you have something written about doctors?" Or, "Do you have a writing sample about law?"

The reason my agent does this every year is that he is trying to get me hired to write a movie, or is trying to get me a position as a writer on a television show. He can't do that without a good inventory of writing samples from me. If you want to get an agent and get a paid writing assignment, you need to have a good inventory of writing samples, too.

ABOUT SCREENWRITING CONTESTS

Are screenwriting contests worth the time, money, and effort to enter? Do they get your scripts read and noticed? Well, it depends.

For someone who lives outside Los Angeles and New York and has an amazing script, these contests are a good way to get some recognition and encouragement. However, in the 17 years I've been a screenwriter, I have never met anyone who has won a screenwriting contest. Nor do I know anyone who knows anyone.

I think these contests are of value to hopeful screenplay writers who want to put up their work and measure it against others. I have never heard of it opening any doors, though it is a way to get your script read by someone (I'm not sure who).

Again, I have been on three television shows, done countless writing assignments, and never had anyone say, "Hey Sterling, this is Mark. He won the Atlanta screenwriters award." It's tremendously popular, but the big producers I've known don't give a damn.

Now there is an exception—film festival shorts. I have seen directors rise up from the ranks by making a kick-ass short that gets attention at the larger festival competitions.

If you exhaust the above scenarios, there are no guarantees, but it will at least increase your chances of making it from Idaho to Hollywood.

FILM IS THE DIRECTOR'S MEDIUM; TELEVISION IS THE WRITER'S MEDIUM.

If you are just starting out and want to work as a writer, turn your head in the direction of where there is the most work for writers—television.

My first break in the screenwriting business was the pitch I made to a Columbia Pictures executive mentioned earlier in the Chapter "How to Pitch". I wasn't prepared. I had no idea what I was doing. I had no credits, and no experience. I landed an agent based on a screenplay I'd written on spec (speculation). This means I made the story up. It was not assigned to me.

The Columbia Pictures executive stared at me for what felt like an eternity. He then picked up his telephone and made a call. I heard him say he had a young man in his office with a good idea for a movie. He hung up the phone and told me to go home and write the story. That's how I made my first $40,000 as a Hollywood screenwriter. It was my first, accidental pitch.

Even though the movie *Gus* was never made, I began to receive more meetings, I met more people in the industry, and before I knew it, I was a working screenwriter in feature films.

For the first five years of my career, rewrites were all I seemed to do. I discovered I had a knack for being able to read a screenplay, and immediately knew how to fix it. I had no idea where this gift came from. I didn't learn it in college. I never went to film school. But there I was, doing re-write after re-write of feature film scripts. Most of the films were never made. I received no credit for the ones that did get made, but I gained experience, credibility, a good reputation, industry contacts, and lots of money.

During this time, I met a man who became my greatest mentor, Robert Greenwald. He taught me a lot about writing. He knew I had good instincts, and he had the courage and generosity to hire me for three or four films for television called "movies of the week," or MOW.

Robert Greenwald helped me carve out a very steady diet of MOW writing, mostly re-writes. One day, after several months of careful tutelage, Robert pulled me to the side and told me that I was the best kept secret in Hollywood. I knew it was a compliment, but I wanted to be more than just a best kept secret.

This was a seminal moment in my career. I was grateful for all the work and mentoring he had given me, but I wanted to do more. I didn't want to be a secret.

Transitioning into television writing helped put me on the map, and opened even more doors for me. It has opened the doors for many other writers, too.

One day, a few years back, I ran into an old friend who had written and produced a play starring Jenifer Lewis. The night the play premiered, I went along as my friend's guest. The play was outstanding, and Jenifer Lewis was incredible.

I was invited to the after party—a small Hollywood gathering with the usual known stars and faces. My friend introduced me to many people. He politely heralded me as new feature writer on the rise to great things. *Note*: This was at such a time that being a feature writer somehow had more cache than television writers. The playing field had not yet been leveled or superseded by HBO or Showtime or TNT, etc.

I made my way around the party with my nose perched in the air a tad. After all, CAA (Creative Artists Agency, a premiere industry talent agency) had said I was the next "August Wilson" and future bright star. So when I met a woman who introduced herself as a playwright from

New York, it was not enough pop to turn my big head her way. Then she told me she was interested in writing for television.

Of course, this was the deal breaker. Feature film writers were a high breed of animal. How could this lowly, wannabe television writer even dare strike up a conversation with the next August Wilson? I slowly gave her my back and found some corner to strike a pose like a Michelangelo statue.

Now, here is where I so brilliantly connect the dots and explain why this story is being told. This particular woman I snubbed went on to create a little television show called *Friends.* She now makes more money than I can calculate, and she has long forgotten my name or even meeting me.

Aside from the lessons of "never burn any bridges in this town" and "don't let your ego get big enough to trip you," one of the lessons from this story is to write for television. The fact that television writing has now become more "elevated" in status has nothing to do with it. The fact that you will have a better chance to get your foot in the door in this industry—and get paid to write—is the biggest reason.

I tell this to my students all the time. If you want to be a screenwriter, then write for television. If you want to be a director, then direct film and television. There is nothing wrong with feature film writing, other than feature films are still, and will always be, the director's medium, and television will always be the writer's medium. It's also easier to break into television writing than feature writing.

Every time I finish a feature film writing assignment, the last I hear from anyone on the project is when I turn in my last draft or polish. In television, when you turn in a pilot that someone has purchased, this is only the beginning of a possible ascension into the stratosphere.

One particular writer got a staff writing job on a show. The show was cancelled, and the showrunner put him on another show that had a seven- or eight-year run. The writer was promoted through the ranks from staff writer ($3,000 a week) to executive producer ($25,000 to $35,000 a week). At the end of the show's successful run, the writer-turned-executive producer created two shows. Both shows failed miserably. The writer/executive producer was then given a position as the showrunner on a show that had a successful five-year run. Yes, this writer failed upward.

Television writing is like going to Harvard. It's hard to get in, but when you get in, they keep you from failing. Not in every single case, but yes, television is the writer's medium.

Every year there are about 150 pilots bought and shot. The over and under is only 15 or so. Of those 150 pilots, 20 to 25 shows get picked up and make it to air-time. Each show averages about eight writing positions. Multiply that times 22 shows, and that equals about 176 new writing positions every season. Of all the successful shows, each one loses one to three writers per season to a new show. This creates another plethora of writing positions.

Compare that to feature films. Less than 60 feature movies are made per year. The over and under again is 15 up or down from 60.

Artistically, movies used to be the most prestigious writing. Now with shows such as *The Wire, Big Love, Breaking Bad, House, The Shield, Mad Men, The Sopranos, 24, Lost,* and on and on, television has leveled the playing field, or in some cases, surpassed the big screen. Logically, the bottom line is that television employs more writers than film.

Again, if you want to work and increase your chances for promotion and more work, write for television.

HOLLYWOOD SEASON

Knowing when to shop your scripts around will increase your chances of getting them seen and sold. Some months are far better than others for trying to get your foot in the heavy metal doors of the television world, so it's important to know how the pilot season works in Hollywood. The following schedule is general and does not always apply to cable television.

January, February, and March: Pilot Season

DO: Read pilot scripts, try to sell film scripts, write your pilot script, and try to get an agent if you don't already have one.

DON'T: Try to sell television scripts.

January through March is when network television and some cable shows actually shoot/film the 100 to 160 or so pilots that have already been purchased. It's the busiest time of the year for actors and one of the slowest for writers.

Do not schlep your television script around to sell between January and March. Instead, try to get your hands on all the pilots to read. It will increase your chance of getting a job when the shows are selected. This is also a good time to push your agent to sell your film spec, or get you a writing assignment on a feature film.

Special note: The end of January is Sundance film festival. Do not try to get a meeting with a key decision maker from mid January to the end of January. They are not in town.

April, May, and June: Staffing Season

DO: Try to find a position as an assistant on a show, try to sell film scripts, perfect your pilot script, and get an agent.

DON'T: Try to sell television scripts or get a meeting.

April through June is the staffing season for the shows that will be picked up for May sweeps. Between 20 to 30 shows make it to air. You may be selected to join a television show, but that show may be cancelled before you get to take your seat in the writers' room.

I worked on a new one hour drama, and we wrote and shot eight episodes before we were pulled from the air. Only five of the episodes made it to air time.

This is a very hard time to get a meeting as a beginning writer. All agencies are working like rabid dogs to get their current clients (writers) a writing position on a show. This is a good time to try to find a position as an assistant on a show.

Pray that you win the lottery and find work on a show. If you have not been called by June, it is time to push your agent to get a feature film writing assignment, or make them sell that spec script you've been working on for 12 years.

July, August, and September: Mid-season Replacements

DO: Try to sell your pilot—push your agent to sell, sell, sell; if you don't have an agent, get one now.

DON'T: Sit around wishing upon a star, or focus on film scripts.

This is the time for mid-season replacements. The shows that didn't make it past sweeps need to be replaced. This means there is a frenzy to buy new pilots. Have your pilot finished and in perfect shape. Try to get an agent; if you have one, push him or her to sell, sell, sell.

October and November: Buying Frenzy

DO: Get your pilot in line and sell it.

DON'T: Procrastinate, think your script isn't good enough, or focus on film scripts.

The magic month of November is my favorite month as a writer because it's the best time to sell a pilot and/or a feature film script. Every year there is a buying frenzy for feature films and television pilots during this time, and writers need to know it and work it.

Read the trades in November. You will see deal after deal being made. This is because most companies need to spend the rest of their money before the end of the fiscal year. Why? Because if a production company receives funding and does not spend it all, they will not receive the same amount the following year. If they received 20 million dollars in funding and only spend 15 million, then the following year they will only receive 15 million. They have a vested interest in buying scripts in November to spend their money.

I have been tortured by stories from production accountants and attorneys who have told me how many bad scripts get bought up in November. Try to get your good script in front of those bad scripts.

December: Break/Get Some Rest

DO: Enjoy the holiday season, even if you don't celebrate a holiday.

DON'T: Expect anyone in Hollywood to take calls or meetings this month.

'Nuff said.

GETTING FIRED—EXPECT IT

An experienced writer from *ER* and *West Wing* told me that everyone in Hollywood gets fired, especially writers. He told me this when we were both writers on a hit television show.

After one full season on the show, I progressed from not knowing what I was doing to being told at the end of the year that the creator of the show said my last episode was the best episode of the year. I was proud and flattered. I was also fired.

I was on another show and met a writer I really liked. When our show was cancelled, we kept in touch through e-mail and text. We met a few times for drinks, coffee, or a quick bite. We did our best to be supportive of each other in those lean or unemployed times. We both eventually found work.

My writer friend landed on one of the most talked about high-profiled and critically-acclaimed one-hour dramas. He wrote an episode nominated for a Golden Globe. His reward? He did not receive an invitation to the Golden Globes, and when his episode won the award, he was fired.

I also knew a writer who created a show that became a number one hit. The show went on to last past the coveted five-season syndication. The writer who created this hit show was fired from his own show during the first season.

Was there any rhyme or reason why my writer friends and I were fired off shows after we had proven ourselves as worthy writers? It makes no sense, but it is a common story. Maybe someone with power felt threatened. Maybe somebody didn't like our cologne. Who knows? There was simply no logical reason why we should have been fired—yet we were.

The truth is writers get hired and fired all the time for no good reason. Television and film writers are often deemed as disposable as tissues. There are a plethora of theories behind this unjustifiable phenomenon; each theory has been overly discussed among writers and with our therapists. Nothing makes us feel better about it.

The only thing we writers can do about it is accept that it comes with the territory—and not let it bruise our egos or stop us from moving forward. Every writer who has survived, or not been fired, is either protected by a divine power, or has the ability to keep his or her head down and go unnoticed.

I have never been able to go unnoticed. I have always been susceptible to firing because my mouth has been too loud or too quiet. On one show, I was once told by an executive producer that the creator of the show complained to her that I was too nice. This has always been a problem for me. When it comes down to being too nice or outright rude, I will always choose too nice. I was reared to believe manners and friendliness are commodities as precious as gold. If someone doesn't appreciate that, I would rather not work for him or her.

My only advice is to keep your head up if you are fired from a job. Another job will eventually come along.

Part of getting another writing job is working closely with your agent. But unfortunately, the "getting fired" phenomenon also extends to our representation.

I have fired my agent, and my agent has fired me. No matter who does the firing, it all comes down to economics. If a writer stops earning money, his or her agent must move onto greener (monetary) pastures. If the writer makes no money for the agency, the writer must go. Conversely, if the agent isn't getting the writer into the doors of decision makers, the agent must go. It's business, not personal (but it feels personal).

Sometimes an agency will fire a writer from sheer guilt of not being able to find work for the writer. Many agents fire the writer because they are underachieving for the writer and do not want to be accountable for their own incompetence. Other agents really hustle and get meetings for their clients (writers), but ultimately the writer is not "making the sale." It's an important partnership; both parties need to do their part.

Writing for television and film is a business wracked with fear and lack of accountability. Everyone wants to point the finger at the other person for failure. Unfortunately for television and film writers, we are too often the last person to point the finger toward. It's just part of the deal—best to know that going in.

OPTIONS AND DEALS

Everywhere I teach a seminar or workshop, several writers tell me they have "optioned this and optioned that." These phrases are tossed around like verbs. Usually, I will nod and say something polite. Then I will quickly walk away, to keep from discussing it any further. I hear so many of these ill-fated scenarios; any advice is lost on the hungry and eager writer.

An option is when someone wants the right to shop your story or screenplay for a certain amount of time. There are various options, ranging from free or $1 to $50,000. There are so many variables that it would take a lifetime to study all the options. They are vast and obscure.

So, let's nip this in the bud.

The first question to ask someone who desires to option your script or idea is if they are guild signatory. This question means are they a part of the WGA (Writer's Guild of America). If they are not, then expect Pandora's Box.

I have heard of situations where writers signed away an option for five years, yet received no money. Most amateur screenwriters are so happy anyone on the planet is interested in their idea or screenplay, that they are willing to let it go for nothing—for eternity. This is usually the case with non-guild signatory producers (wannabe producers).

The next question is whether you, the writer, have an entertainment lawyer? No, not a friend of a friend whose cousin is a real estate lawyer and once saw *The Sound of Music.* Do you, the writer, have a real entertainment lawyer? Entertainment lawyers draw up contracts for screenplays and ideas. This is their specialty. This is what they do all day long.

If the answers to these two questions are "no," then good luck and good night. You should work with guild signatory producers for your own best protection, you should get paid for any option, and you should definitely have an entertainment lawyer to be your cage in shark-infested waters.

What is a standard, reasonable option? I'll tell you, but I know you will argue all day long if you are not a professional screenwriter with an entertainment lawyer. A standard, reasonable option is $5,000 to $40,000 for six to 18 months, with a considerable increase to re-up (renew) the option.

The last time I optioned a screenplay was for $10,000 for 12 months, with a re-up for $50,000 for an additional 12 months. "Yes, but, yes, but ...," you say. This is the standard, reasonable option for an idea or a screenplay for a guild signatory production company. Whether you can get it or not depends on your entertainment attorney and your own belief that you are a damn good writer and a professional one at that.

If you don't have an entertainment attorney or an attitude that you should get paid for your work, again, good luck and good night.

By the way, famous writers and directors receive far more than this standard.

Now, if a ridiculously famous and successful studio or network wants to shop your idea or screenplay for free for an eternity, it's up to you. At least you have read the standard option agreement and it will only increase in time.

THE "IF COME" DEAL

A lot of reputable producers, networks, and studios will offer you an "If Come Deal."

It is a written contract that is professionally negotiated on your behalf. This means that if the network or studio sells your project, your deal is already in place. You have to be willing to partner with the producer, network, or studio. Everyone agrees to try to sell your project together. They become your partners. Again, a contract has been signed and agreed upon.

WHAT IS A DEAL?

Whereas an option is the right to "shop around" your screenplay or idea, a deal means someone wants to buy your screenplay or idea, or hire you as a writer for a show or project. A deal is the settlement you receive upon rigorous negotiation by your agent or entertainment lawyer for your screenplay or services.

It is usually called a "three-step deal," but it is nothing remotely "three step." The three steps are as follows: a first draft, a re-write, and a polish. You (the writer) will be paid a percentage of the negotiated fee already signed and sealed.

Even though it's called a "three-step deal," it is never really three steps. Who knows why it's called that anymore. Once the ink is dry, this is the ballpark standard deal. The writer receives a commencement fee for his or her services (often including an outline). This means the writer has been hired, a contract has been signed by all parties, and the writer is on his or her way to a meeting to begin the work at hand.

The next step is to be paid for delivery of a first draft. If you are worth your weight in gold, the first draft you turn in better not be your true first "crappy" draft, but the draft you feel best represents a solid first draft. For me, that's usually three drafts.

Then you (the writer) receive notes from a story meeting or conference call. You are then asked to go off and attend to those notes.

Now you finish, come back, and turn in a second draft. If you are worth your weight in gold, this better not be your true draft number two, but probably draft number five. By now, you are smart enough to know that "three steps" has flown out the window. Including outlines and true drafts, we are up to at least six to seven steps.

Now the producers, network, and studio are feeling good, and feel you can bring this project home with a super fine polish. Yes, we are on the seventh or eighth step of the deal, and we are now calling it a polish. If you are worth your weight in gold, you know that the polish is supposed to go into production with full crew and staff.

This, my fellow screenwriters, is called a "deal" or officially—a "three-step deal." Please note that payment for all these steps is as arduous and insurmountable as climbing Mount Everest in bare feet in the middle of a snow storm. Not only do you need a great agent, manager, and entertainment lawyer to receive payments, you also need to be best friends with a Bengal tiger who attacks on command.

Hey, nobody ever said it was easy. Well, at least not the pros. But when you do get the option, the deal, and finally the check, I'd say it's very well worth it.

AM I SMART ENOUGH TO WRITE A SCRIPT?

Once in a while someone asks me, "Do you have to be smart to write scripts?"

The answer is, "Not really." You have to be a good storyteller, a good salesperson, good at learning certain skills (structure, etc.), and good at common sense social skills, but you don't have to be a Harvard graduate.

When I first started getting paid to write screenplays, I would stand by the front window each day waiting for the fraud police to arrive in their fraud cars, bust down my front door, clap their fraud handcuffs on me, and haul me to fraud prison. I kept thinking that I wasn't smart enough to get paid for my stories and ideas. Then something happened that altered my perceptions I had about my intellect as a writer.

The agency that inquired about and fielded offers had placed me on the Hollywood screenwriting map. In fact, job offers poured in, and I wanted them all. One day I received a call from my agent. "Sterling, you've been approved by Berlosconi," she began, "and they're offering you $100,000 to write *The Black Princess.*"

"That's great."

"Are you sure you want to do it?"

"You bet your boots."

"Sterling, can I be honest with you?"

"Of course, you said you'd always be honest."

"You haven't finished the *Dance Theater of Harlem*."

"That's right, but I'm all over it."

"Sterling, that's four jobs you'll be doing at the same time."

"Is there a problem?"

"Yes, you're spreading yourself thin. You're going to have to learn how to say 'no.'"

"Lucy," I retorted, "the two years of PB and J sandwiches for breakfast, lunch, and dinner have compelled me to take every job that comes my way."

"Yes, I understand, but if you don't put your best foot forward on each job, you may not get hired again."

Pause, thinking. So, $100,000, huh? I sat in my apartment wondering how I was going to deliver any of the scripts in such a short time frame. And then a lightning bolt struck: I was going to get a writing partner. I picked up the telephone and called my good friend who was senior legal counsel for one of the "big three letter agencies," ICM (International Creative Management).

"Hey, Joshua."

"Hey, Sterling, what's up?"

"Josh, I'm getting a lot of jobs. I can't keep up unless I get a writing partner."

"Wow. What a coincidence."

"What?"

"I was just on the phone with my cousin," Joshua continued, "you know, the one who graduated number one in his class at Harvard Law School. He's the one I told you who won the $100,000 grand prize on Jeopardy."

"Oh, yeah."

"Well, he just told me he'd love to meet a young working writer who may need or want a writing partner."

"Number one in his class at Harvard Law School?"

"Yeah, the kid's a genius. You want me to set up a meeting? You'll love the guy."

"Absolutely."

Three days later, I was sitting in front of Joshua's cousin, Ethan. I kept my poise, but Ethan appeared to me like a miniature Michael Creighton, scary smart and scary good looking. The guy graduated number one in his class from Harvard Law School, and then decided to pick up some extra cash by winning the grand championship of Jeopardy.

There I sat, the "B" student from St. Mary's College who paid more attention to sports, martial arts, and girls than class work. I wasn't sure if I wanted a writing partner who was so gifted—and a potential matinee idol.

"Ethan."

"Yeah?"

"Dude, you're like a cross between Albert Einstein and Cary Grant. Are you sure you want to be a ghostwriter?"

"Yeah, I mean, I eventually want to write my own stuff, but it'd be cool to learn from someone in the biz."

Pause, thinking that standing next to this guy, I may never get a date again. "Cool," I replied. "So, how do you want to work this?"

"I don't know, Sterling. Maybe you should read one of my scripts first."

Pause. The genius matinee idol has already written a script?

"Have you written a script?"

"Actually, I wrote two," he grinned. "Here, take them home and give them a read."

"Cool."

So, Einstein scripts in hand, I sat in front of fireplace shaking in my boots. I decided to put my fear and intimidation under the sofa cushion, and I read the first script.

I sat there puzzled and bewildered. Something was wrong. Maybe this script was just a really rough draft. He was just warming me up for what was going to be the read of my life. I opened the second script, read it.

I put both the scripts down and wondered if I had ever read anything so nonsensical and horrible in my life. Actually, no, I had not—at least not with the high expectations I brought to the reading. Both scripts were horrendous. How could this be? Number one from Harvard Law School and Jeopardy Grand Champion, yet these scripts were atrocious. It took me a couple days to get up the nerve to call him.

"Hello, Ethan?"

"Hey, Sterling."

"Yeah, so listen ..."—*the doctor just told me I've got this little condition called leprosy. And it's really super contagious, so we can't work together.*

"What?"

"Um, I was thinking maybe I should go it alone."

"You don't want a writing partner?"

"Well, I was thinking ..."—*I should find a writing partner who can actually write.*

"Excuse me?"

"What I'm trying to say is that I wish I had gone to law school. Man, you have the brightest future."

"What did you think of my scripts?"

Pause, thinking. *I think you're one of the worst writers on the planet.* "I thought they were okay. You've got a lot of potential."

"Thanks."

"You're welcome."

I hung up the telephone and sat in awe. The Einstein model had taught me one of the biggest lessons I ever learned about screenwriting: Being smart doesn't mean you can write cinematically. Writing screenplays demands particular skills. You have to learn them. Just because your IQ might be off the charts doesn't mean you can write feature films or teleplays.

Man, was I relieved. I wasn't the smartest guy in the world, but I understood how to tell a story. Maybe I had a future in writing after all.

And maybe, just maybe, so do you.

HOW TO GET YOUR SCRIPT READ

In the old days, someone could pick up the phone and say, "Hi, Sid, this is Nancy. You're an agent, right?"

Pause. "Yes, Nancy, I'm an agent. I've got million dollar clients and lots of toys. What can I do for you?"

"Actually, Sid, my cousin's son is a screenwriter, and I heard he was good, even gifted."

"No worries; fly him out, send him in, and I'll take care of him. He'll have a three-pilot deal by the end of the week."

"Thanks, Sid. You're the best."

"No worries, Nancy. Call any time."

These fantasy days are long gone, and these types of stories are all linked under the same category now: prehistoric.

When I first started writing screenplays, all you had to do was write well, tell someone you know you wrote a script, and then the universe would shift enough for your script to fall into the hands of someone who cared and could do something about it. This is exactly how it went for me:

The telephone rings.

"Hello?"

"Sterling."

"Yeah, Micah."

"I heard you wrote another script."

"You heard right."

"Dude, you've got balls. Matt said your first script was a stinker."

"It was."

"So, when can I read the new one?"

"Try never."

"Dude, come on. I'm one of your best friends."

"Micah, you are one of my best friends. But a secret keeper, you are not."

"Sterling, come on, dude. Let me read it."

"Okay, Micah. But I swear, if you let one single person read one single syllable, I will hunt you down and strangle you with my bare hands."

"Geez, dude, just let me read the damn script. I'll tell you if it's a stinker."

"Okay, but for your eyes only, right?"

"Sterling, you worry way too much."

I send him the script. Two days later the phone rings.

"Hello, this is Sterling."

"Can you hold for Michael Besman?"

Clueless. "Okay."

Pause.

"Hello, Sterling?"

"Yes."

"This is Michael Besman, Senior Vice President of Tri-Star Pictures."

Holy cow. "Yes?"

"When can you come in and talk about the script Micah gave me?"

Okay people, this is no lie. I remember it as if it was yesterday. How could I forget my first meeting with a big studio executive? That was how easy it was back during the days when dinosaurs roamed the earth. Today, getting your script read is harder than ever. The portal closes more and more each day. One day soon, there will be an atom named "chances of getting your script read."

People ask me all the time, "How do I get my script read by someone at least remotely connected to the industry?" Here's how you do it.

First, write a great script. Not a good or decent script. Write a great script. Somehow, what shows up on the page eventually can't be denied when you've written a great script. Try to find a way to make that same great script a pilot sample. Feature scripts are read at least 95 percent less often than pilots.

Reminder: If you want to be a screenwriter, write for television—it's the fastest way to get you in the door.

I know I've already said it before in this book, but it's worth saying again (as I say it again and again to my students): Television is the screenwriter's medium; feature film is the director's medium. Most of my students manage to ignore this simple, undeniable fact, until they become desperate to be employed as a screenwriter.

There are more than 160 pilots sold every year. Very few of them make it to the air, but you only need to sell one to get into the game. And if you don't sell your great pilot, you have a good chance of getting an agent, manager, or a job, if it is truly good.

Features don't work that way. If you write the perfect feature script, you will not see a dime until it has been through the malaise of gauntlets all perched to shred any hopes of it getting to a big name producer, director, or actor. If your feature gets that far, then it will be successful only when all the biggest players are attached and signed, and the money is in place. The odds of all these elements falling into place are the same as standing on your lawn, flapping your arms, and flying to the moon.

Write the perfect feature film, and then start flapping your arms. See which happens first, a sale or landing on the moon. I bet it will at least be close.

NOW THAT YOU'VE WRITTEN THE SCRIPT

So, you've written a great screenplay and you have turned it into a great pilot, here is what you do. The best option takes a lot of eating humble pie.

Find a working screenwriter with an agent. Tell him or her you wrote the best screenplay in the world, and you want to piggyback off him or her to get it read.

What does this mean? It means you are willing to include the working writer's name on the title page. Either give him or her co-writer credit, or give him or her "story by" credit.

I was approached to read a script, was blown away by it, took the script to my agent, introductions were made, and a new super-talented writer was launched. If your script is that great, very few working writers will turn you down. And very few working writers' agents will turn you down. But this scenario relies on the assumption that your script is great.

Personally, I have piggybacked at least three young writers into stardom. This is why: A great script never makes anyone look bad. Yes, all writers want the world of screenwriting to be about them and only them. But a great script makes everyone look good. Yes, it might annoy an agent or manager when another name shows up on their client's screenplay. But if it is truly a great script, agents and managers see dollar signs.

All right, so you don't know one single working writer and you wrote a great script. Go find an assistant on a television show or a development person and beg him or her to read your script. Most assistants on television shows are the next working writers on that show. They have nothing to lose or gain by reading your script, unless it's a really bad script. In that case, they will hunt you down, or totally ignore you in the future, because they will never get that valuable time back.

Assistants have power. The reason they got their jobs as assistants is because they are related to someone powerful, which makes them powerful. The other reason they have power is that someone powerful was sweet on them enough to hire them. Now they run that powerful person's life. If they tell their powerful boss they read a great script, that powerful boss will read the script before the end of the week.

All right, so you don't know an assistant. Find a development person at the producer, studio, or network level. The development person's sole mission in life is to find a great script for as cheap as possible and get it to his or her boss. Find the head of development or assistant head of development of any film or television company, and send him or her lots of cookies, candies, and beverages of their choice. Sweet-talk the person until he or she concedes to reading your great script.

(*Reminder note:* No one reads more than five to 10 pages of any script unless it grabs the reader. Great scripts grab the reader within three to five pages.)

All right, so you don't know any working writers or assistants or development people. You are on your last leg. Here's what you do: Go do some intensive research and find an upstart literary manager. Note—not an established literary manager, but one on the verge of breaking out. The reason these managers are not established and only on the verge are that they are looking for the next great script. How do you find them? By doing massive amounts of investigating and inquiry.

Young managers are hungry, and they are the few creatures who need a great screenplay in order for the other elements and dreams of their lives to fall into place, including big money, a big house, a big office, and marriage to the big supermodel.

GETTING AN AGENT

NOTE: A lot of this chapter will read the same as the last.

I have been a WGA member for nearly 20 years. The business of getting an agent and being an agent has changed over the years. It used to be that every agent was in the business to take chances on new talent and build an empire around that new talent. Today, agents are only in the business to find working talent more work. Taking a chance on new talent is prehistoric. The only chance today's agent is willing to take is in the effort to steal other fully established talent from competing agencies.

Why did it change? It's hard to say. In the past, the filmmakers ran the business of film. These people were bold, brazen, and trailblazing, and believed the only things that mattered were the stories and how they came to life on screen. Profit margin was an afterthought to great cinema. Now, profit margin is the bottom line. The stories are a distant after-thought.

Now, corporations and media giants run the film business. What matters to these conglomerates is box office revenue. The television and film industry is now fear-based—fear of no profit is the driving force behind all decisions. Therefore, new, unproven talent isn't worth the risk. Only established talent gives the corporate giants the best chance to make money.

My first agents saw my potential, and felt I was able to bring them a revenue stream from my writing. They forecasted the revenue stream would increase over time because as my credits grew, so would my ability to negotiate bigger writing jobs and earn more money. They were right. On my first official job I earned $40,000. Within a year I was earning more than $200,000. None of this would have happened if two hungry agents were not willing to recognize my talent and take a chance on me.

WORK YOUR WAY UP TO GET NOTICED

While working on two successful television shows I witnessed firsthand the protocol of ascending through the ranks. It goes like this:

Get a job on a television show as a PA (personal assistant), which, simply stated, is grunt work. You pick up and deliver everything from scripts to items that are stored in the writing room kitchen. From this overworked and underpaid position, you may get lucky if the stars align and earn a promotion to the next level up—assistant.

Assistants answer phones and schedule and re-schedule appointments for executives. When you are a proven assistant, you can set your sights on becoming a staff writer.

Every season, the studio or network hires someone outside the writers' room to write an episode. It is a way to save money. The first in line for that assignment is usually the assistant. The first television show I worked on, two assistants were given an episode each to co-write with a higher-level writer. Both of those assistants went on to become full-time staff writers. Presently, they are both producers.

If you are in the queue to be a staff writer, believe me, agents will be interested in you.

FINDING A HUNGRY MANAGER OR AGENT

I mentioned that one way to get your script read is to piggy-back your script with an established writer. This is also a great way to get the attention of an agent. If your script is brilliant, an established writer will ask, "What would you like me to do with this?" The answer is to ask the established writer if he or she would be willing to come on as a co-writer, or offer to share story credit. Agents will notice.

The next way of getting an agent is to find a manager who is trying to build a reputation through managing talent and producing. My first manager launched my career. After a big studio executive read my script, he wanted to know who was representing me. I had no representation. A phone call was made, and a few introductions later I met Sharona Fay, a manager who was just starting out. She carted my script all over town until there was a small legion of agents who were impressed with my scriptwriting and wanted to meet me.

Making countless calls to promote and arrange meetings for a client is exactly what a good manager does. A good writer shows up with a stellar script, an impressive inventory, a great pitch—and makes the sale.

There is a belief in Hollywood that warrants some truth: the only time you need a manager is when you are so unknown no one is willing to give you a chance, or when you are so big, you can't keep up with the demands of your time.

I cannot stress how important it is to meet a hungry manager. This is one of the last lines of getting an agent. Two of the best managers I've had put me with an agent and helped the agent shepherd my career. Why agents don't do this themselves is another story.

NETWORK AND PLEAD TO READ

Another way to get an agent is a repeat of advice in the chapter "How to Get your Script Read." Find an assistant on a television show, and beg him or her to read your script. And/or get out there and network in Hollywood circles-- you're bound to trip over one.

Finally, the last strategy is to find a development person at a producer, studio, or network level. If your script is undeniably magnificent, the development person will notify his or her employer and you will get a meeting—this alone will attract the curiosity of agents. That meeting will not necessarily result in the sale of your script or a writing assignment, but it guarantees you have been officially put on a list of writers to consider.

If you are lucky enough to get a meeting with a studio, network, or reputable producer or production company, call around to agents *before* the meeting, let them know you have an upcoming meeting with the (big name), and tell them you are seeking representation. The fact that you have secured a meeting with such a big name will intrigue them. Hustle to get an agent before the meeting, because no matter how brilliant you are, you will need representation before any big name will buy a script from you, or hire you.

When you get a meeting and that door of opportunity is open, be positive in your presentation. You must also continue to write, and write well. The standard of your writing that got you the meeting must be upheld to sustain interest in you. It is up to you to keep the door open with relentless effort.

The previously mentioned steps to getting an agent are in no way guaranteed, but what is guaranteed is that these steps will put you in a better position than you are at present. Unless you are the son or daughter of a mega star, executive producer, line producer, camera operator, director, cinematographer, agent, casting agent, director, or editor, then forego all of the above and pester your mom or dad.

WHAT'S IT LIKE TO BE A SCREENWRITER?

When people ask me, "What's it like to be a professional screenwriter?" my answer has always been the same. More than a dozen years ago, back in the days of PB & J sandwiches and Top Ramen, my partner—who has since achieved super power, fame, and fortune—and I sold a speculation script (called a *spec*) to Disney. My writing partner was working as an assistant at one of the big three-letter agencies, making less than $20,000 a year. I was working on becoming a screenwriter. I was making zero dollars.

Our deal was to the tune of "325 against 450." This meant we would see $325,000 of $450,000 to see the spec through the steps of commencement (i.e., the delivery of a first draft, rewrites, and polish). If our script somehow made it into production, the remaining $125,000 had to be given to us within 10 days from the start of principal photography. This is why all writers pray their scripts make it to production.

THE FIRST DRAFT

Our unspoken agreement was always that he would start the script and then I'd fix it. We were a good team.

The idea for the screenplay came to me in a dream. I pitched it to my partner. He liked it so much he said he would start the first draft. We delivered the script to our agent on a Wednesday. Thursday morning our agent called and said she thought we had hit a home run. Friday the script was sent to four or five producers. Tuesday morning we received a preemptive offer from a big name producer who had a deal with Disney.

She wanted us to take the script off the market so Disney wouldn't have to deal with a bidding war. At that point in our careers, we were unwilling to take the risk of turning down such a big opportunity and simply hoping there would be other offers, so we accepted the offer. Needless to say, we were a couple of happy writers.

On the following Thursday, we received our first check, the customary seven percent of the 325 against 450. On the next day, my partner quit his job in order to focus on writing. I had nothing to quit except poverty.

Our first "notes" meeting was scheduled. When my partner and I walked toward the large executive building at Disney, he asked me, "How do you want this to go?"

I answered, "Remember what former Notre Dame football coach Lou Holtz said to one of his players after the player did a back flip in the end zone?"

"What'd he say?"

"Son, the next time you score a touchdown, act like you've been there before."

We stopped, flashed cool smiles, did the celebratory smooth dap, and continued toward our new future.

We entered the conference room. There were two interns with pen and note pad. The president of the production company, Chris, sat before us, and we exchanged the usual polite preamble before getting to business.

"Congratulations on writing a great script."

"Thank you."

"How long did it take for you guys to write this?"

My partner and I looked at one another. I said, "Five weeks."

Eyebrows raised in respective amazement all around the room. "Impressive."

"Thanks."

"Thanks."

"Listen, fellas, let's cut to the quick. We love this script. We want to make this movie." We suppressed our smiles. "However, we want the next draft to be a lot darker."

My partner and I nodded. No worries, we got this.

So Chris gave us suggestions on how to make the script a little "darker," a little "smokier." We all shook hands. My partner and I were off.

REWRITES #2 and #3

Two days later we called our agent to tell her we were done with the notes. She told us to wait five weeks and then deliver. Two days was not long enough to make the big wigs feel as if we had worked hard enough.

Five weeks later, we waited in the conference room for Chris. We knew we had hit another home run. The rewrite was indeed dark and smoky.

Chris never entered the room. Another person, Sharon, entered the room. Chris had taken a job with 20th Century Fox. The new president of production was now Sharon. She tapped her pen on the table, sized us up, and said, "Guys, we love the rewrite. But it's too dark."

My partner and I refrained from stealing a glance at one another. We returned to the drawing board and, three days later, we brought the script down a notch. It was less dark; it was mocha. We were proud of the work.

Five weeks later, we again sat in the conference room, eager to receive the rest of our $325,000 (minus the customary seven percent they had paid us in advance). We surveyed the room for Sharon, but the new president of production, Susan, arrived and told us Sharon had gone elsewhere. My partner and I avoided looking at each other. We twisted in our seats and listened.

"Guys, love the script, but we want to bring it back to the original version."

My writing partner and I looked incredulously look at one another.

We failed to deliver our next draft in five weeks. We were distracted; we had spent the money we'd earned so far. Then one morning, we arrived at the coffee machine at the same time. We both nursed hangovers.

My partner looked at me and said, "We have a meeting on Wednesday."

"Why?"

"The polish of our script."

"You've got to be kidding. I'm ready to stick a fork in my eyes."

A long, very pregnant pause followed, with some morning scratching. I looked down on the counter and saw an unopened letter from Turner Pictures.

"What's that?"

"I don't know, dude; I just went to the mailbox."

"It's got both our names on it." I opened the envelope and pulled out two separate checks written to my partner and me. The checks were for $50,000 each. We looked at each other and did a perfect celebratory dap.

"Nice."

The production office had moved from Disney to Turner Pictures. Their moving expenses included a $100,000 re-up to keep our script.

REWRITE #4

We arrived to unfamiliar surroundings, with a new conference room and new employees. At this point, we were not surprised that Susan had moved on. Neither of us flinched when the receptionist said, "John will be right with you."

John, the new president of production, was really a cool head. He was easygoing with the looks of a model. The only reason he never modeled was that he wasn't even in the zip code of six feet tall. My partner and I looked down at him and politely shook his hand as he said, "Love the script, guys."

"Thanks."

John scrambled for notes that never existed.

"I particularly like the scene when Bobby Jones…"
I couldn't resist, "Billy Ray."

John was a little thrown but kept his composure. "Yeah, Billy Ray. Loved the scene outside the church."

I had to ask, "John, have you read our screenplay?"

John gave us the deer-in-headlights look. My partner and I stole a glance at one another. The non-verbal communication between us indicated one more meeting like this and we were going to do something unplanned and really bad. We had approached a year since our first story meeting with Chris. We had done four re-writes for four different presidents of production.

WHAT'S IT LIKE?

When I'm asked what it's like to be a professional screenwriter, I always share this story, flash a coy smile, and say, "I'm actually in the business of re-writing."

Yes, it's often frustrating, maddening, and like a roller coaster. But it's also exciting and thrilling, and, to me, far better than a lifetime in an office cubicle *not* screenwriting.

(*Note:* The feature scriptwriting world is not remotely the same today as depicted here. A writer sees no money until all the "A" list players are on board and financing is in place. That means there is no scratch for two to three years. Maybe a stipend for the right to shop your script, but today, studios spit in your open hand and tell you to kiss their butts.)

STORIES FROM THE WRITERS' ROOM

My first one-hour television show aged me 20 years each month. The show had a lot of pressure and expectations from the studio and network. The co-creator of the show was one of the most influential writers of our era. The showrunner (and creator) had created and was still supervising one of the most successful one-hour shows in the history of cable television.

The fear on that particular television show was that the showrunner/creator was going to get bored and wander back to playwriting. The studio and network were also afraid the co-creator was going to be overwhelmed and opt out of his commitment.

The studio and network decided to stack the deck. They filled the writers' room with some of the top executive producers and co-executive producers from award-winning shows. In the world of *Star Trek*, it would be a room full of Captain Kirks, plus one guy in the red shirt (me).

On this show, the writers were expected to not only write brilliant episodes (otherwise you would get fired—no joke), but to also produce our episodes. This meant we had to complete a written episode within one week or less.

Once the showrunner signed off on the episode, it was sent to the studio and the network. Then we were to sit in on notes from the studio and the network for changes to the script. We then had to re-write and complete our episodes within a day or two days after the notes. After completion of the studio and the network notes, we had to have a word with the most important person on the set.

The most important person was not the creator, studio, showrunner, or network. It was the line producer, as it is on any television show. The line producer is the one who sticks his or her head in your office and says things like:

"Sterling. You know that scene you wrote where the car falls off the pier into the water?"

"Yeah."

"Get rid of that scene."

"But it's the most pivotal scene in the episode. It's the nail-biting act out of the teaser."

"I don't give a rat's ass. There is no budget for a pier, water, or car. Next time you write that shit, you're fired."

"Well, okay."

"By the way, great script. I love this episode."

"Thanks."

Once the changes were made from the line producer's delicate suggestions, we then had to sit in on the first table read. This is where the actors get together and read the script out loud for the first time. We had to make adjustments after the lead actors finished their whispers to the showrunner. The whispers were usually dialogue changes, which usually had to be incorporated into the script.

After the table read, we went to the technical and location scouts. We answered questions from the Prop Master (the person responsible for getting every item for the set, from watches and computers, to everything listed in each scene). We met the director of the episode and sat in on casting (for secondary roles). When the episode began filming, we met with the actors, watched filming, and answered questions from the script supervisor and line producer. After our episode was wrapped, we were not asked to sit in on all the editing sessions, but the editors made sure they found us at lunch to ask us questions, or tell us what scenes had to be cut.

My second show was sort of a watered-down version of the first show I worked on. We didn't exactly produce our episodes or participate from start to finish, but the showrunner would often ask us to go to the set or see the editor.

On my third show, if we (the writers) even considered going to the set, we were automatically fired. The legendary creator of my third television show felt the writer's only piece of business was to write.

Having been an active part of the production of my scripts on my first two shows, *not* being able to be on set was a big change for me. I didn't like it. The writers were all given a blueprint of the show, but not encouraged to go near the set. In fact, we were told we could not go within 100 feet of the set—like a restraining order. Well, everyone seemed to manage this restraining order but me. I wasn't able to imagine the set from a blueprint.

Not one to always follow the rules, I marched up to one of the co-executive producers and asked him if he would like to sneak onto the set with me. I specifically picked this particular co-executive producer to join me in my little mutiny because he had written nearly every episode of the first season of another super hit show, and had won an Emmy for his efforts. I knew he was not only brilliant, but fearless.

Somewhere between lunch break and the next writers' room session, the co-executive producer and I ventured onto the set. We were stopped by one of the set builders or assistant directors. She asked what we were doing and who we were. I stood frozen in terror. The fearless co-executive producer said, "We're writers, and we wanted to see the set."

"You're writers and you've never seen the set?"

"Actually, I'm a co-executive producer and I just wanted to know what happened to the red couch."

"What red couch?"

"The red couch the creator yelled at me for describing as a blue couch."

She just shrugged and moved on. No armed guards came to drag us away. No men in black ushered us into the great beyond. No director or executive producer threatened to fire us for daring to step on set (though it could've happened).

Every television writers' room is different, every writer's story is different, and there are no sure-fire rules.

So yes, I mean no, there isn't a manual—it's all trial and error. Get used to it.

THE MISSING WRITER'S MANUAL

No books, articles, or mentors prepared me for my first experience in a writers' room on a successful one-hour drama. There was no manual. It was my first day in a television writers' room, and I had no idea what to say or do. I had no frame of reference or knowledge about how to ask key questions that may have saved my job and promoted my career. Following are some questions and answers that would have helped me.

Q: What is the pecking order of the room? Or better stated: Who really runs the writers' room?

A: Survey the room and quickly figure out what the pecking order is (i.e., who is the ally or enemy of the showrunner or the creator), and always side with the ally. Always avoid the enemies of the showrunner. The enemies usually consist of any writer who was not directly hired by the showrunner. You think I'm being too strong in using the word 'enemies'? I'm not.

Q: Which award-winning executive producers should I make damn sure not to contradict or step on, after they speak?

A: It's always a good idea to *never* make a decision-maker look bad in front of peers in any business—especially this one. If you disagree with something, bring it up privately, or not at all. Remember, nobody is bulletproof in this industry. I thought a mentor and award-winning executive producer was bulletproof on one of the shows I worked on, but she got fired because someone under her was related to the creator (never underestimate the power of nepotism).

Q: Whose jokes should I laugh at and whose jokes should I only cast a small grin?

A: You think I'm kidding with this question, but I'm not. Ego is big in this industry, and you don't want to be a buffoon or outshine a big peacock. One show I worked on had a writer consultant who was one of the funniest people, in person and on the page, I ever met. He so upstaged the showrunner that the writer consultant was asked not to come to the writers' room any more. It's a delicate balance every writer must learn.

Q: Does the writers' room encourage participation from lower level writers? Or is this a room that will summon the guillotine if I speak?

A: One show I worked on encouraged everyone to speak. Another show never wanted lower level writers to speak. The writers who survived the latter show never, ever participated verbally in the writers' room.

Q: Should I make sure my idea is perfect before I open my mouth, or can I think out loud and hope some genius in the room will carry my gem of an idea to the Promised Land?

A: Unless you are the top dog (as in, own the show), I highly recommend thinking things through before opening your mouth. Once, I painfully spoke out of turn and spoke before the thoughts really formulated in my head. An executive producer dragged me to the side and told me that nobody has time to listen to me try to formulate a sentence, and if I didn't have something valuable and quick to say, to keep my mouth shut. Ouch.

Q: Should I act aloof?

A: Be yourself, but mind the unspoken rules of the room. On one of the shows I worked on, the showrunner would stare off into space for 20 or 30 minutes. All the other writers had to wait. This showrunner was a genius. He proved it over and over again on all the shows he ran. However, it is hard to watch someone think for a half an hour or more, and nobody but the showrunner would get away with it. So don't carry aloof to an extreme, but don't act like an overeager puppy dog that's never been there, done that before (even if you are).

Q: Should I head-bob with zealous approval of every word spoken, even if I feel like vomiting from the absolute worst suggestion I've ever heard in my life?

A: Never head-bob. Listen without prejudice. Stare intently, but show no reaction. Everyone assumes you are smart until your actions (or mouth) prove otherwise.

Q: Should I open a note pad and take notes?

A: Generally, no. You walk into any writers' room and you can tell who has been on shows before. Those are the writers staring at the white board, thinking. I worked with David Mamet and I wrote down everything he ever said. The other writers thought I was a kiss-ass. You generally don't want to be thought of as that.

Q: Are current events important in the writers' room? Should I start reading the New York Times?

A: The best writers' room I ever worked in was loaded with the most intimidating, impressive writers assembled at one time. Every morning, the first hour was spent talking about politics or *Dancing with the Stars*—a show I still have never seen. It's always good to be able to contribute intelligently to a conversation, so it's a good idea to keep up with current news, events, and popular entertainment.

Q: Is this a joke-telling writers' room? Or is this a strictly political-satire-only writers' room? Should I have watched Jon Stewart or Anderson Cooper last night?

A: All writers tell funny jokes and stories. Make sure you only use the jokes that always guarantee a laugh. Also, if you want to be a writer with a modicum of success, then watch very little television. If you want to be a super successful television writer, watch as much television as you can. And for heaven's sake, watch the credits. All the writers listed in the credits will be your future bosses. Trust me.

Q: *When I have no idea what anyone is talking about, should I raise my hand and scream, "I have no idea what anyone is talking about?"*

A: Never. I did that once. The cold stares and deadly silence cured me of making that mistake again.

FINAL SUGGESTIONS

Yes, as you clever readers have figured out, there are many nail-biting considerations when you first enter the writers' room. Many writers get fired from their first writing job because they don't understand some of these implicit criteria. This is what happened to me.

Just remember some important tips for your first television job in the writers' room:

- Never step on the wrong person in the room. Quiet is more respected than nervous chatter. I nervously chattered through my first two shows. My third show I had brought it down to a dull roar.

- Develop your Houdini skills. Contribute in the writers' room if it is required, but remain relatively anonymous. Write brilliantly, but try not to stand out.

- Find the assassin in the room and make friends with him or her. The assassin is the person who plots to get anyone fired who may get in the way of his or her will (i.e., the assassin's promotion). I worked on a show where the assassin started out as the showrunner's assistant. After a few years, the assassin managed to get everyone fired, including the showrunner who gave him his first job.

- Figure out if the writers' room wants your audio contribution or not. On one show I worked on, verbal contribution was a good way to secure your future on the show. Another show I worked on really encouraged new writers not to speak. First-time writers on a television show often overcompensate by nervously speaking in an untimely fashion. I should know, because I did that on all the shows I worked on. I was so eager to contribute in the writers' room that I nervously spoke out of turn, and also said things that were not remotely related to the discussion at hand. It didn't help me at all.

I once asked a co-executive producer how he had managed to survive on two or three top-ten shows. He said, "Write perfectly and keep your head down."

That sums it up beautifully.

DON'T GET TOO SMUG

It took me two years of writing and meetings to get noticed as a screenwriter, and nearly two more years before I made my first big mistake as a screenwriter.

The first two years seemed insufferably long. I spent long hours reading screenplays and how-to books on writing screenplays. I typed and typed into the wee hours of the morning, fueled by hope and naïveté. The only thing I had going for me was the undeniable fact that I knew I wasn't the smartest or the best (yet), but I knew I would be the last to quit. Perseverance is essential for success in this industry, and I'm really good at it.

The initial review of the first screenplay I wrote read something like, "Dude, this is terrible." (By the way, it's normal to write a "crappy first screenplay," so give yourself permission to write it and then move on to a better one.)

I trashed that screenplay and began writing my second screenplay, which garnered far better "Man, great screenplay" reviews. In fact, this second screenplay captured the attention of the respectable big three-letter agencies. This is a big deal—like the Holy Grail. Many writers have to leap several small agencies in several long bounds before getting noticed by "the big three," so I was feeling pretty good. It had been two years of PB & J sandwiches, but the two years had passed relatively fast. As quickly as a bad blind date that lasted two years.

THE BIG MISTAKE

I met with all the big three-letter agencies and then decided I'd sign with one of them. All I had to do was go see one last, small agency, which I had no intention of signing with for this project. Two women with the same first name managed this particular agency.

I stared at my fingernails while both women told me what I already knew: I had talent. The other larger, big three-letter agencies had told me so. When I was about to leave, the two women with the same first name said something that made me stop in my tracks: "We understand you've already spoken with the other larger, big three-letter agencies. We just want you to know that we will read everything you write and give you our honest opinions."

I stood there with both shoulders pointed toward the front door. The other larger, big three-letter agencies never said anything about opinions or honesty. My budding ego was (thankfully) overshadowed by common sense. I slowly turned back to the two women with the same first name and asked, "Where do I sign?"

Those first two years with the small agency, managed by the two women with the same first name, were (to date) the most prosperous years of my career. I made more money and worked more often than I ever have as a professional writer. In fact, one of the women told me with no uncertainty, "Sterling, you're going to have to learn how to turn down job offers."

When I heard this, I thought she was out of her head. Was she flat crazy? Learn how to turn down jobs when I had starved for two years? "Hell no," I wasn't going to turn down anything. I wasn't even going to turn down a special invitation to meet with the other largest, most feared and most notable three-letter agency in town when they extended it to me.

This was soon to be my first big mistake as a professional screenplay writer.

REFLECTING ON CHOICES

How could I have avoided the mistake of trading in the small, success-magnet "David" agency for the large and highly impressive "Goliath" agency? At the time, with the honor and ego that came along with recognition from the star-studded Goliath, it was impossible.

When a big three-letter agency comes calling, every writer, actor, director, and producer responds. All of us initially fear that the first time the big three-letter agency calls on us might be the last time they call on us.

My only defense was that the invitation to meet with the largest, big three-letter agency came on the heels of being notified that the two women with the same first name were parting ways. They each were going to start new agencies. Each asked me to come with her, but the other largest, big three-letter agency beckoned. My destiny was already written in stone.

The largest, big three-letter agency had invited me to their seduction chamber, the Peninsula Hotel. No writer could resist the temptation to leave his or her last agency while getting served $10 glasses of hot tea and $15 croissants. It was intoxicating. One hot tea and a croissant for $25! Give me that pen. "Where do I sign?"

During the honeymoon stage, the largest, big three-letter agency gripped me with every phone call. They had me when I stepped into that famous building. They really had me when I laid eyes on my script with the largest, big three-letter agency's logo on the cover. I had died and gone to heaven. I used every single opportunity to tell anyone and everyone that I was now represented by the largest, big three-letter agency.

"Hi, Mr. Anderson, shave and a haircut today?"

"Did I tell you I signed with the largest, big three-letter agency?"

"Are you ready to be seated?"

"Did I tell you...?"

"Would you like fries with that hamburger?"

"Did I tell you...?"

"Son, are you coming home to see your mom on Mothers' Day?"

"Hey Dad, did I tell you I signed with the largest, big three-letter agency?"

"You can take the largest, big three-letter bleep and shove it up your largest, big three-letter bleep, if you don't make it home for Mothers' Day!"

The second you are unemployed and need someone to beat pavement to find you another job is the exact second the largest, big three-letter agency calls you, because you've, for the hundredth time, called to ask why they (the largest, big three-letter agency) stopped calling.

"Hello."

"Hello, Sterling?'

"Oh, gawd, I'm so glad you called. I just put on my shoes to go jump off a bridge."

"Actually, that's why we are calling."

"Really."

"Yes, hope you can swim. Good luck with the career."

Click. Dial tone.

EPIPHANY

It took another nearly two years to get back in the game after the largest, big three-letter agency dropped me. During that time, I called one of the two women with the same first name. This was the one who started a new agency that is now one of the most notable mid-size agencies in Hollywood, with a long list of successful clients.

"Hi, this is Sterling Anderson. Remember me? I was just calling to ask if..."

Click.

"Hello? Hello? Is anyone there?"

Dial tone.

The moral of this story is, if a small agency signs you and you are constantly working, do not get too smug and accept any invitations for a $25 hot tea and croissant.

HOW TO DEAL WITH BAD PRODUCERS

When a new writer breaks into the consciousness of the producers and agents who can do something for the writer's career, he or she is launched into the inevitable "development hell." This is where I had my first encounter with what I call a "bad producer," and this is where I learned my first lesson on how to deal with a bad producer.

Actually, I have three stories that demonstrate the lesson because, really, you need to know. If you ever start getting paid to write screenplays, you will eventually run into a bad producer, and this information might either get or save a paycheck for you.

But before you meet good or bad producers, you must navigate development hell.

DEVELOPMENT HELL

I was launched into development hell after I signed with my first agent.

Development hell begins when a literary agent or manager sends a newly signed screenwriter around town to be introduced to all the producers the agent or manager knows. These meetings, called "generals," are usually with men and women referred to as "development." These people take appointments with hot, new writers, and they must know all the new and old writing talent in town. General meetings are arranged primarily to establish relationships, or listen to new pitches and ideas for pilots and movies.

After I signed with my first agent, I had 53 meetings in three months with development people. Believe me, after 30 meetings in two months, you tire of the same routine, beginning with perfunctory handshakes and politeness.

"Please, have a seat."

"Thanks."

"Did Pat ask you if you wanted some water or coffee?"

"Yes, thank you."

"Great."

Pause. Hmmm.

"So, tell us a little about yourself."

"Well, I played sports in high school. Went to college on academic and athletic scholarship,"—*where I discovered the only thing I was interested in was getting laid and going to parties.* "And I began to study writing."

"Nice."

"Thank you."

"So, how did you arrive at writing this brilliant screenplay your agent (or manager) sent over?"

"It's a long story, really. The short version is I wrote a script I could use only for toilet paper. After that, I wrote another script, although I told my good friend if he showed it to anyone I would kill him in his sleep."

Pause. Raised eyebrow.

"I only say 'I would kill him in his sleep' because, awake, he's actually one tough hombre."

Pause.

Quickly glancing at his or her watch, "So, the script..."

"Oh, yeah, so I wrote this script, put everything I had into it."

"I really enjoyed it."

"Thanks."

Pause.

Then the inevitable question always, always asked, "So, are you working on anything you'd like to talk about or submit to us?"

This is a development person's true job description: get the best idea from an unknown writer for as cheap as possible.

"Well, I'm kind of working on something that is a little like *Transformers* meets *Modern Family* meets *Lost*, that sort of transitions into a cop, buddy, romantic thriller."

Raised eyebrow. Genuine interest.

"Sounds great. Can you have your agent send it over?"

I nod, unsure. Did I just give away the goods or bluff my way into a possible meeting with this person's boss, who is the only one who can actually write a check?

"Yeah, sure."

The development person looks at his or her watch. Eleven a.m. Only 10 more meetings, and these people can call it a day.

"It was really great meeting you." The development person extends a hand.

I nearly fell over the table because I felt as if I had just blown any opportunity to come back again. I stared at the extended hand wondering if it was my breath, the booger in my nose, or the absolutely most unintelligible pitch ever given in the history of the world.

I finally offered a wet, sticky, trembling handshake. "Thanks."

"Do you have a parking ticket to validate?"

No, I actually parked 16 blocks away because I only have two nickels to rub together and I didn't want to risk getting stuck with a $16 parking garage bill.

"Excuse me? Ah, no thank you, I found a meter on the street."

The development person gives me a pat on the back, unrelated to warmth or kindness. And I leave.

You can see why, after 50-plus of these meetings in three months, this process is called development hell. Of course, mixed into the malaise of meetings come several invitations to coffee, drinks, breakfast, dinner, or golf. And along the way, it's inevitable to run into a bad producer.

BAD PRODUCER #1

Somewhere in these meetings came one of my first experiences with a really annoying person, who I now call a bad producer. I was 20 minutes into the meeting when I felt the walls closing in.

This vice president of creative development blathered on so seamlessly that he sounded like the trumpeting voice of the teacher in Charlie Brown animations. I soon discovered the guy was one of the most self-centered, self-entitled, pompous, narcissistic knuckleheads I'd ever met. I stopped paying attention somewhere around his indifference to the homeless or animals. The last three minutes of the meeting a mantra repeated in my head: "You're the biggest ass I ever met, and I really just want to give you the finger and leave."

"Wah, wah, wah, I am great. Wah, wah, my movies were the greatest ever made, wah, wah." On and on and on.

Two minutes and counting, I wanted to rip his lips off. One minute and counting, my knees bounced with fury. My clenched fist made my knuckles protrude and turn white.

That was it, so I stood and said, "Thank you for taking the time to meet with me. You really are a gem."

He smiled and shook my hand. I turned and went out the door. Even in my car, an internal voice cried, "Just go back and give him a little slap in the face. What could it hurt?"

The next day I stood before the newspaper stand, contemplating going into therapy to talk about my inexplicable disgust for this man. I glanced down at *Variety* and the *Reporter* (two notable trade publications), and noticed the bold writing: The pompous jerk who I wanted to maim was now the "Newly Appointed President of a Major Studio."

I couldn't believe my eyes. Needless to say, insulting or assaulting the guy in any form would have resulted in my excommunication from Hollywood.

At that exact moment, I realized I would never utter a profane or critical word to anyone. Lesson learned and kept.

BAD PRODUCER #2

The second bad producer I met appeared a few years later. My then-girlfriend and I invited him over for dinner because I wanted her to meet the first producer who ever stood over my shoulder and dictated what he wanted me to write. I spent countless hours at his home in the Hollywood Hills, often staring at him in disbelief.

I typed, "The man walked down the sidewalk."

"No, no, no, Sterling, that's not it," he said, breathing down my neck from his vulture-like position behind me as I worked. "I said the man *ambled* down the sidewalk."

I remember staring at this producer with my fingers just over the keyboard of my laptop, desperately trying to set him on fire with my eyes.

"Seriously?"

"Yeah, the man ambled, not walked, down the sidewalk."

When I left his home and drove down the hill, I remember doing something I had never done in my career as a screenwriter: I called the studio and asked for the executive of the movie project.

"Art (not his real name), this is Sterling."

"Hey, Sterling, how is the project coming along?"

Pause. I took a deep breath. "Actually, Art, that's why I'm calling. You see, the guy is a wannabe writer, to the tune of giving me dictation."

A long silence.

"Art?"

"Oh, yeah, Sterling. We must have a bad connection. I thought you said he was giving you dictation."

"You heard right. The guy is mistaking me for a court stenographer."

I thought I heard the sound of waves crashing the seashore, but it was just another really long silence.

"Really?"

"Really."

"That's not good."

"Yeah."

"I'll get him on the phone immediately."

"Art?"

"Yes?"

"When you immediately get off the phone with him, will I still have a job?"

"Let's hope."

"Oh, man, Art. I really need the money."

"Don't worry. I'm sure it will work out."

Six weeks later, I completed the script. The entire movie was dictated to me. It was such a painful event, I begged my girlfriend, a gourmet cook, to invite him over just so she could take a look at him.

The dinner was great. The producer who had caused me nearly 10 aneurysms was the most likable guy in the world. His only flaw was that he was a failed writer, and dictating to a writer was the only way he could get his thoughts on the page.

Again, I chose the high road. The result of my patience was that I collected a $70,000 fee, plus a $20,000 production bonus. A marginal film eventually came out, yet I received no less than $10,000 a year in residuals for five consecutive years. No exaggeration. It pays—literally—to be patient and accommodating (within reason).

ONE FINAL LESSON

If reading this short story about bad producers has not screamed a big message regarding what to do when you meet a bad producer, let me provide one more *story*.

I will spare you details and give you the Cliff notes. I passed on a movie project because I wasn't getting good vibes from the producers. The movie grossed close to

$200,000,000 domestically, and became one of the biggest sleeper hits in the past 20 years. Years later, one of the producers always gave me a sinister smile when we ran into one another, although he eventually bought a television pilot from me.

The bottom line? When you get a bad producer and you are getting paid, send him or her lots of love from the universe before every notes meeting, keep your mouth closed, and do your very best.

MEMORABLE BLUNDERS

When I was a younger man, working in wineries in the Napa Valley I had the good fortune to mentor under a couple noted and respected Wine icons, Joseph Phelps and Robert Mondavi. Though I did not have the good fortune to spend all my waking hours with either of the two men, they were both generous with their time and guidance. Mr. Phelps and Mr. Mondavi each said the same thing "You learn more from your mistakes than your successes."

As a winemaker for nearly a decade I was taught 'To know good wine you have to drink a lot of bad wine.' I learned on the job by all my failures how to make good wine. One day I was awarded the gold medal for my chardonnay. It was a long journey and I had made a lot of undrinkable wine before I was awarded that gold medal.

The same can apply to film and television. I had the good fortune to learn a lot from my mistakes as a screenwriter. Believe me, there was a lot of learning because I made a lot of mistakes. I was fired more than a half dozen times and one respectable producer said I was the worst writer he'd ever hired.

There are too many to count but I did have a couple catastrophic blunders I'd like to share.

The first catastrophic blunder happened earlier in my career. I was called into a successful production office at Paramount Pictures. There were two producers that were partners, named Cort and Madden. They were as charming as they were successful. They had done movies like 'Runaway Bride' and 'The Associate' to name a few.

In our first meet and greet meeting they told me that they were working on a movie concept and they were not talking to any other writers. They wanted me to develop with them. I was deeply flattered. They told me the idea and for some reason it did not click for me. Nothing resonated. I was having a really bad brain cell day that extended into a couple weeks at which time I was to return with a thoroughly plotted story concept. When Cort and Madden called my agent to schedule a return meeting, I returned well enough with nothing. My excuse was I had not grasps their basic idea (pitch to me.) I told them I wasn't sure if they were doing 'Fame' or 'Guess Who's Coming to Dinner.'

So politely, I passed on the project. The truth was I did not step up to the plate and take my swings. I chickened out. I did not prepare. I had an opportunity and I whiffed.

Cort and Madden were forced to move on to a different writer. It happened to be some numbskull who had the audacity to flush out a pretty good story.

Months later, I stopped looking at the box office totals for 'Save the Last Dance' (somewhere around 125 million dollars domestically) and it took several more months to stop crying.

Through the subsequent years, I have had a number of meetings with one of the above-mentioned producers, and he became one of my favorite people in Hollywood. I may be reading into it, but he always seems to have a small, coy smile, when I'm in his office.

The second major blunder happened much later in my screenwriting career, when I had a lot more credits and experience. I had made the IMDB (International Movie Data Base) and not as a fabricated 'consulting writer' but with solid sole credits. This did not necessarily preclude me from having other brain freezes though. The second terrific blunder was even worse than the first but I had the experience and I knew better to let an opportunity slip through my fingers.

I was called into a Disney division to discuss a movie concept they had bought. I was confused because it was a comedy and I am not a comedy writer. I sat down with a creative development producer who was even smarter than she was fetching. I found myself thinking more in terms of setting her up on a blind date with my friend than I was hearing the concept.

You see, it all started wrong. The women's good looks was more my focus than landing the job.

She told me that they had bought a pitch and needed a writer to flush out the story. I was in the room because someone at Disney loved my writing and believed I could deliver the goods.

The beautiful creative development producer explained the concept they had purchased like this, "There is going to be a wedding and the groom is going to Vegas with his buddies for a bachelor party. The only catch is the groom cannot drink because he has a horrible reaction to alcohol and it literally turns him into the devil. When they return from the bachelor party things start happening that none of the men can explain. The week of the party, dangerous bikers and mafia men show up looking for the stolen money. The groom had married a stripper hooker and the mayhem gets worse by the minute."

I went away to mull over the concept and I came back, but with only half an effort of a flushed out well developed story, and predictably the beautiful creative development producer passed on me.

I can even remember the look of disappointment in her eyes while I spit out a half-baked concept for a story.

Now that 'Hangover' has made a gazillion dollars I'm back into therapy – it makes sense to me to seek out therapy in lieu of yet another crying jag.

Obviously the concept was developed by more adept comedy writers than me. The movie is one of my all time favorites.

The reason I am sharing these two blunders is not to brag about how big a man on campus I am or to impress. I share these two blunders to explain that many wannabe writers believe they are too far away from the opportunities and no one will ever give them a chance. The truth is there is no guarantee you will not have failures when you finally get your chance.

All in all, I have few regrets in my career. I have sold screenplays, worked with Academy Award winning actors and actresses, Emmy and Academy Award winning producers, and a Pulitzer Prize winning writer.

I have helped foster the careers of now noted writers. As the adage goes, when you take the elevator to the top floor, you must always send it back down.

And one of the biggest rewards for my focus and perseverance was a writing assignment I will never forget.

One of my greatest mentors, Robert Greenwald, hired me to right the story about the three wives of coveted civil rights leaders, Medgar Evers, Dr. Martin Luther King Jr., and Malcolm X.

After sitting in Coretta Scott King's kitchen listening to her regale me with what courage it took to change civil rights in America, I can't complain at all.

FAVORITE SCREENWRITING STORY

As a screenwriting instructor and guest lecturer at film schools and colleges, the one consistent question has been: If you could only share one story in your 20-plus years as a television and film writer, what would it be?

The question always rattles my brain because there were countless stories I would want to tell. Narrowing it down to one might seem implausible.

The time Sidney Poitier took me out to dinner and regaled me with stories about his life behind his academy award winning films. Maybe.

The time I was brought into the showrunner's office at the end of the first season of an immensely successful new hit series to be told the creator of the show voted my episode the best of the year. Possible.

Getting a personal, hand written letter, from the president of a major network, congratulating me that my MOW (movie of the week) was one of the highest rated movies of the week in the history of the network. Good chance.

The list goes on and on, and I have shared most of them and will continue to share.

However, if I only could tell only one Hollywood screenwriting story, it would be the story that happened on a one-hour television show I was hired to write for that was cancelled after only eight episodes.

The pilot was coveted as one of the best pilots in recent history. I was honored to be one of the eight writers picked to join the show.

Unfortunately for the creators of the show, the network, and all of us writers, the lead actress tested very poorly after the airing of the first episode.

None of us writers were deterred but we all knew there was trouble in Denmark.

No matter how brilliant the writing, directing and editing the lead actress got worse and worse. Our ratings dropped and dropped. We were on a sinking ship and we all knew it. We knew the main culprit was the lead actress. She was terrible and to add insult to injury she had no chemistry with the lead actor.

The creators of the show called the writers into the room and told us the good news and the bad news. The good news was the creators of the show had convinced one of the most successful actors in television history to jump in and join our show. All the writers were thrilled. The successful television actor was not only a great actor he was also a great person. Cheers to him (wink.)

The bad news was, the successful television actor was not going to be written into the show for two or three more episodes. First we had to write the actress he was replacing off the show. We had to write in her assassination.

Here is where the plot thickened.

We all knew that when the floundering lead actress was notified of her exit ticket off the show, she was not going to show up on the set and let us film her assassination. She was going to stick it to us because we planned on sticking it to her. Her tremendous ego wouldn't allow her to cooperate with us.

So, we (the creators, the network, and the writers) were all stuck, right? Wrong.

One of the writers (unfortunately not myself) suggested we not tell the lead actress we were writing her off the show. He suggested we write a sequence where she is shot and then wakes up to realize it was only a dream.

When the next episode was re-written the lead actress was thrilled she was going to be such a large part of the episode. In fact, the dream sequence of her being shot was going to give her extra footage and screen time. She was delighted.

Little did she realize the dream sequence was never going to be televised. What was going to be televised was the footage we now had. We now had footage of her assassination. We were now able to tell her she was going to be fired off the show.

As anticipated when the lead actress told she was going to be written off the show and replace she refused to be any part of the next couple episodes. She indeed walked off the set.

No worries, right? So we thought. We had the footage of her assassination.

The successful television actor joined our show and all was well. Unfortunately, the damage was already done. Our ratings had dropped beyond repair. Even the successful television actor was not able to repair the wreckage. The show was cancelled.

However, I had witnessed and been part of the most diabolical but ingenious way to assassinate a character off the show without them knowing it. This is and remains my favorite Hollywood screenwriting story.

FINAL THOUGHTS

Like many unfortunate children in America, the only bequeathment from my biological father was abandonment.

After two years of dating, my 20-year-old pregnant mother went to her 42-year old boyfriend, a cop, and said, "I'm pregnant."

The cop answered, "I'm married."

I like to share this with my USC film school screenwriting students because often when I stand in front of them at the beginning of each semester, the only thing they know about me is what is written in the IMDB (Internet Movie Database).

They know I somehow ventured to Hollywood and was able to magically meet and work with the best of the best. They come to know that David Mamet taught me how to write. That Sidney Poitier taught me class and dignity outranks most human qualities. That Robert Greenwald taught me you're no one unless you give back to the unfortunate and underprivileged. And that Coretta Scott King sat in her kitchen and told me stories of immeasurable fortitude.

So every semester I stand in front of my students, and they assume I was born into literary nobility. They think I must have been child protégé who quoted Shakespeare at the age of two, and was plucked from an elite group of young boys and girls with silver spoons in their mouths. Or they assume I am the cousin, brother, or nephew of some famous African-American producer, director, or film star.

So after everyone settles, positions their computers at the ready, turns off their cell phones, and gives me their undivided attention, I gaze into each of their eyes and say the same thing every single first class of every semester.

Clearing my throat, I say, "I'm a living example that each and every one of you can make it in Hollywood at whatever you choose or desire to do, no matter what your background or circumstances."

This is met by silence and nervously roaming eyes, so I tell them a story from my childhood:

One of my first vivid childhood memories was when I was four years old. It was an early morning in Tuskegee, Alabama, and it was already hot as an oven and humid as a sauna.

A small fan blew in every room, of which there were not many. That night the unmerciful, sweltering heat decided not to break from the hottest part of the day. Instead, it knocked on the door when the sun went down. When I opened the door, it barged inside and found a place right under the sheet with me as I tried to sleep. I wanted to sleep, but the heat wanted me to stay up all night. All I was able to do was kick off the sticky, wet sheet and beg the heat not to come back tomorrow, but I knew it would.

I slept on a rollaway cot positioned just shy of the front door. One morning, after sweating a good portion of my body weight, my bowels were doing a two-step, so I rolled off the cot and made the trek to the back of the house.

My eyes were barely open when I pushed open the back screen door. I started down the steps, paying little mind to my Uncle Red, who was in his familiar early morning position—passed out on the back porch swing. An empty liquor bottle rested beneath his outstretched hand. Some mornings when I was more bright-eyed, and the devil sat on my small shoulder, I'd catch a fly and put it in his open mouth. Seeing my uncle cough and sputter was almost worth the price of him running me down and whooping my behind. This particular morning, even the devil was too hot to play.

I found the hole in my briefs, scratched my behind, and sauntered toward the outhouse. I saw Uncle Red's truck. It was partially through the hedge, and the front door was still open. The hedge was Uncle Red's way of knowing when to stop in the wee hours of the morning. He'd hit the hedge, the truck would stall, and he'd tumble out of the front seat. When I finally learned to tell time, Uncle Red's truck crashing into the hedge was how I knew it was three in the morning.

I opened the outhouse door. The squeak in the hinges cried, "Please oil me."

I lifted the toilet seat. The flies flew up through the seat, danced around my head, and celebrated the early releases from the stench of the outhouse hole. I tore some pages from a phone book, pulled down my briefs, and sat down. I swatted at the flies circling my face.

The sound of a broken pipe or a punctured tire startled me. My eyes widened, because I knew that sound was neither a tire nor a broken pipe. I looked in the corner and saw a black water moccasin, coiled and hissing at me. Whatever the snake was trying to communicate didn't remotely sounded like, "Top of the morning to you."

I flew out the door and my briefs came off as I raced toward the house. I flew up the back porch steps and jetted past Uncle Red. The sweet smell of cologne and bourbon hit my nose, even though I was approaching 90 miles an hour.

After telling this story, I turn my back to my students' wide open mouths and start writing on the chalkboard.

The point I try to make to all of my students is that I was born with no chance of writing a movie which would star remarkable actors and actresses such as Sidney Poitier, Mary-Louise Parker, Diane Wiest, George Newbern, or Lynn Whitfield. No one told me I could be a doctor, lawyer, scientist, or have a shot to work with legendary writers like David Mamet, Glen Gordon Caron, or Shawn Ryan.

Statistically, I had an 80 percent chance of not completing college, and a 40 percent chance of going to jail or prison. This is why I do not believe in statistics. This is why I am never able to look anyone in the eye and say, "It's too hard. You have no shot." Because I know it's not true.

I know writers are told all the time how impossible it is to break into Hollywood. I know you are told the odds are against you. I know connections are important and most people get jobs in this and any other business by "knowing someone" (that's why networking and working on small projects when you start out is important), and that nepotism runs unfairly rampant. I know what it's like to be on the outside looking in, and it's sometimes hard and unfair.

If that's what you want to concentrate on, go work in a cubicle somewhere. But if you can trash these excuses and try anyway, you have a chance. I know you *can* make it; it *is* possible! If you are persistent and have talent, you *will* shine and succeed. It's not just a pep talk—I've lived it.

By the grace of God, my journey to get to where I am today pales in comparison to the journey my parents had to take to get me here. Both my mother and stepfather were born into stifling segregation and oppression. Neither of them was allowed to go to white schools, shop at white stores, or eat at white restaurants. They drank from "colored only" fountains, rode in the back of the bus, and were told to accept the confines of their generation.

Somewhere in my childhood, my parents dedicated themselves to making my life better than the life they had growing up. They made a decision to take my brother and me out of the segregated, poverty stricken south—and they taught me to not just accept any confines, but to break through them and rise above them.

Every single person who has the dream of becoming a screenwriter can fulfill that dream. It takes work, discipline, and a stalwart belief in yourself. And finally, it has to show up on the page.

If you can transfer your talent to the page for the next successful movie or TV show, you will be a big hit, no matter what your personal story. I know—I did it. So can you.

ABOUT STERLING

Sterling Norman Anderson is an award-winning, Emmy-nominated screenwriter of more than 20 years.

He has written for some of the most popular network television shows, such as *The Unit* on CBS, as well as NBC's *Medium* and *Heist*. His teleplay *The Simple Life of Noah Dearborn*, written for CBS starring Sidney Poitier, received three Emmy nominations and won an Image Award. Sterling's extensive resume also includes screenplays written for Lions Gate, Disney, HBO, TriStar Pictures and Columbia Pictures.

A graduate in English from St. Mary's College, the accomplished writer also spent five years teaching screenwriting courses as an adjunct professor at the USC School of Cinematic Arts.

Sterling's first book, *Does He Cheat?*, is a nonfiction, hair-raising, testiment on infidelity. He has written two books on writing, *Writing Without Fear* (2010) and *Beyond Screenwriting* (out on Kindle and releasing September 1, 2011 in paperback). The author often guest lectures and panels on screenwriting at film schools and festivals across the country.

Born in Cincinnati, Ohio, Sterling spent his early childhood in Tuskegee, Alabama, before moving to Davis, California. He writes from Los Angeles today. His talents span far outside the world of writing. Sterling has a fifth degree black belt in Tae Kwon Do and was an award-winning winemaker in Napa Valley.